MORE TRADE...

WINEMAKERS ON JAKE LORENZO....

"Jake forces us to face that most dangerous, yet beguiling of all adversaries--ourselves. To follow Jake down this difficult, but rewarding path is to see a little into one's own conscience...."

Bob Sessions
Hanzell Vineyards

"Exciting, thought-provoking, highly entertaining. Jake's approach goes from light-hearted to heartfelt concern for people, wine, and the quality of life..."

Richard Arrowood
Arrowood Winery

"Jake Lorenzo is a private investigator. His best investigations are of the human character."

Jim Bundschu
Gundlach Bundschu Winery

"Until you've seen him wrapped in plastic and surrounded by four gorgeous women wielding paint brushes, you'll never know the real Jake Lorenzo."

Michael Jones
Domaine Chandon

"If Jake Lorenzo didn't exist, we'd have to invent him."

Lance Cutler
The Cutler Cellar

WINE WRITERS ON JAKE LORENZO....

"Old Jake's conscience just keeps itching, and old Jake keeps on making a good show out of scratching it. Good, clear writing on some subjects that need to be talked about just like this."

Bob Thompson
San Francisco Examiner

On the Jake Lorenzo columns... "What can be said to convey their satire, their insight, their color, their sense, their flavor--and all in the six punchy words publishers want for a dust jacket?"

Gerald Asher
Gourmet Magazine

"The blonde walked through the doorway. 'Jake,' she said, a tear in one eye and in a voice as soft as a caress, 'this is a marvelous book. Nobody else writes about wine the way you do. You're funny; you're moving; you're passionate. You make so much sense, Jake, so much common sense about wine. Oh, Jake...'"

Bill St. John
Rocky Mountain News

Cold Surveillance is the best book about wine that I've read in years."

Jerry Henry
WWL Radio, New Orleans

THE WINE TRADE ON JAKE LORENZO....

"Jake's new book is a delightful insider's look at the wine industry. He doesn't pull any punches... Best of all, Jake's fun-loving personality shines through every chapter."

Dan Noreen
Wine Exchange of Sonoma

"If you want to know about the ugly under-belly of politics, read Hunter Thompson. If you want to know about the under-belly of the wine business, read Jake Lorenzo."

Chuy Palacios
Chuy's Burrito Palace

When entering Jake's world, be prepared to feel with your soul and celebrate life without a safety net. Jake's extraction of the extraordinary from the ordinary, his appreciation of laughter and respect for choice and tradition are only attained by trading shoes.

The Monsieur and Catherine the Whole
Toonknockers International

COLD SURVEILLANCE

The Jake Lorenzo Wine Columns

by

Jake Lorenzo

Published by: Wine Patrol Press
                  P.O. Box 228
                  Vineburg, CA 95487 U.S.A.

FIRST WINE PATROL PRESS EDITION, OCTOBER 1993

Library of Congress Cataloging-in-Publication Data

Library of Congress Catalogue Card Number: 93-85259

Lorenzo, Jake. Cold Surveillance: The Jake Lorenzo Wine
Columns/by Jake Lorenzo. --First Edition.
p. cm
ISBN 0-9637438-4-8: $9.95 Softcover

Printed in the United States of America

To my Dad, who through good fortune had a chance to fight, and is here when he might not have been. And to Tracy, who through the vagaries of fate had no chance to fight, and is not here when he should have been.

ACKNOWLEDGEMENTS

Thanks to Lisa Weber. Never has a detective had a better editor.

Chuck House did the cover design which made me realize it was going to happen after all.

Ron Zak, the only man who can photograph whatever I imagine.

George Letteney made this computer illiterate into an electronic wizard. Well, maybe not a wizard. Thanks George, wouldn't have happened without you.

Charles McCabe, for the inspiration and the model.

Thanks to all the people who gave advice, help and encouragement about writing, editing, printing and publishing.

Thanks to all the Toonknockers, especially Catherine and Jerry.

Finally, to Jakelyn and her Mom...thanks, I love you.

CONTENTS

CONTENTS

FOREWORD

Rip off Jake Lorenzo's mask and who do we see? Why, Dionysus himself, of course, ever outrageous, ever exhilarating, ever for freedom without distinction, ever for life at its most intense. Nietzsche borrowed Dionysus to symbolize genius, the force that encourages each one of us to respond to the world freely, in his or her own way. If he'd waited a while he'd have had a better example: Jake Lorenzo.

But world-class philosophers (as we say in California) are always in a rush and always looking for the big deal. Jake Lorenzo isn't a big deal; that's his charm. You can find him most days on the end bar stool at Chuy's Burrito Palace. He's the one in the wine-stained jeans and the scuffed cellar boots, carrying on about a world that sells wine like frozen peas and Wonderbread and then wonders where the magic went.

Gerald Asher
Gourmet Magazine

INTRODUCTION

I was in a tasting room in Sonoma, California. It was at least 90° F, in the shade. A truck pulled up in a cloud of dust, and a shirtless man in cut-off shorts jumped out. "You're Rusty Staub, aren't you?" he said. I replied, "I used to be." We exchanged pleasantries and he said, "You've been tasting wine all day, right?" When I said, "Yes, I have," he told me to come with him.

He reached into the back of his pickup and pulled out a small cooler of ice-cold Budweiser. We walked up to the top of the hill and sat at a table. We drank Bud and talked about wine for a couple of hours.

That was my introduction to Jake Lorenzo. Since then, we've been to some of the swankest and some of the seediest establishments in America. San Francisco, Chicago, Houston, New Orleans, or New York; it made no difference where we were, Jake would sniff around each city deciphering where to go for a good time and great wine. Plus, he was like a guard dog protecting you wherever you decided to go.

It was Jake's chameleon-like ability to relate to different groups that amazed me. His down-to-earth style, his approach to life, and his understanding of winemaking all won me over. I knew if I needed protection, of if I needed something investigated, I could count on Jake. Besides, if we ran out of things to do, we could always get a great bottle of wine or a cold Bud and talk about how the world could be a better place.

I always look forward to my encounters with Jake. I never know what to expect, but that's part of the charm of knowing Jake Lorenzo.

Reading *Cold Surveillance*, I was amazed at Jake's ability to make so much sense about how basic winemaking could be, considering how hard some people make it sound.

I'm in total agreement with Jake when he decries the insane rules and regulations and taxes on wine. And dear God, please let someone get the winemakers of America to tell the public how good the moderate consumption of wine can be for them.

If anyone can do it, it's Jake Lorenzo.

Rusty Staub

PART I

Family
and
Friends

CLOSETS

When Jakelyn's mother and I first got together, we used to argue about closets. She insisted upon cluttering our closet with dresses and coats and pair after pair of shoes, while I recognized that the closet was the coolest spot in our apartment and was therefore the only logical spot for the wine cellar.

Jakelyn's mother was obstinate. No amount of arguing could change her mind. She refused to give up an inch of space. Not one dress, not one skirt, not even her purple and green spike heels would be sacrificed for the wine cellar.

Well, I certainly wasn't going to stop drinking wine. I bought and saved and collected all the wine I could. Whenever I needed more space, I got rid of some of *my* clothes. Soon I was down to three Hawaiian print shirts, one pair of Levis and my high school tennis shoes. Something had to be done.

No amount of learned discussion had swayed her. Threats were ignored. Bribery proved ineffective. Desperate, I went to the store, spent more than I could afford, and brought home the oldest bottle of California cabernet sauvignon I could find. The wine was delicious. Brimming with rich cabernet flavor, set off with the aged mellowness of oak, the wine became a sensuous experience.

Jakelyn's mother loved the wine. That night the purple and green spike heels were missing from the closet.

I relate this ancient domestic tale to illustrate a point: maintenance of a wine cellar is essential if you want full value for your wine purchasing dollar.

3

California winemakers spend enormous amounts of time and money to produce some of the world's finest wines. They take great pains to rush the picked fruit to wineries for crushing. They follow elaborate and costly procedures to prevent any sort of oxidation in the wine. They meticulously fine and filter the wines to achieve just the right balance of fruit and oak and tannin. Then, invariably, they release the wine before it's ready for consumption.

Don't take my word for it. Go to the wineries. Ask the winemakers. Most winemakers feel that three years of aging is the absolute minimum for fine red wine, yet California wineries routinely release red wines just two years after vintage.

Winemakers also agree that every wine needs 4-6 months of bottle aging just to come out of the shock of the bottling process, yet many wineries are forced to release wines just days after they are bottled.

All of this is hard to believe, but in today's wine market time is money and the interest keeps adding up. Wineries simply cannot afford to hold onto their wines. Costs of warehousing, in addition to the interest being charged on that unsold wine are staggering.

By the time that additional cost is passed on to the consumer, wine prices could easily be 25% higher than they are now. With overall wine consumption down, and likely to go lower still, many wineries find themselves in a "cash flow crunch." The last thing the wine industry needs now is a price increase.

Given the current situation, the consumer has just two choices. We can buy the wines as they are released and drink them before they have had proper time to balance themselves. Or we can buy the wines, cellar them, and enjoy them when they have reached their full potential.

Now, don't misunderstand me. I am not advocating that we squirrel away hundreds of cases of wine in dank, dark cellars for decades, only to be disappointed when we find our treasures are over the hill.

I am suggesting that we buy enough wine to put away for a few years to mellow and fill out. Personally, I like to get three or four bottles of each wine I like. I try the first one a year later, and if it seems to be holding up well, I'll wait another year or two before trying the next one. If the wine doesn't seem to be holding up, I drink the others more quickly.

The secret to a decent wine cellar is to have more wine than you can consume in one year. That way, as you continue to buy and replenish stocks, your cellar will grow and age. In any case, each of us has to make our own decisions about how much we buy and how long we choose to hang on to it.

I see that Jakelyn's mother has just tossed out two plaid skirts and that grotesque orange dress she never wore. I'm on my way to the local wine shop to see if I can fill that space.

CHILD REARING

I became a private eye in college. I was more visibly radical in those days, and I learned some powerful lessons that were to influence the rest of my life. The most succinct lessons were administered by the numerous police officers who kept dragging me off to jail at the slightest provocation.

In fact, it was on the day of my first incarceration that I learned my most profound lesson. "Time is the coin of life, be careful lest others spend it for you." Carl Sandberg wrote that. Punctuated by the slamming of a cell door, I took it to heart.

I got a great bail bondsman, known to us regular clients as Lips. Lips afforded me the luxury of freedom, for a price, of course. And with that luxury, I became a private eye, because as a profession it allowed me to invest time as I pleased.

I've dredged up all this past history to discuss my theory of child rearing. My daughter Jakelyn has been a great source of pleasure and frustration. Her mother and I have pretty much played raising her by ear, but early on we did make one major decision.

It is thought, by those who spend life's coins investigating such things, that children learn the patterns by which they will view the world around them at a very early age. By the time a child is four or five, about 90% of the way they will relate to new stimuli is set.

This has always made sense to me, so the only conscious child-rearing decision we made was to be around Jakelyn those first critical years. To that end, I didn't work much. We stayed around the house, or we went to the beach. Whenever we got some cash, we would travel as far as we could for as long as we could.

The theory was that if we provided a safe, solid, loving environment for Jakelyn, while at the same time exposing her to exotic, strange, wonderful visions of the world, she might grow up to accept the unique differences of others. She could view them, not with fear or suspicion, but with fascination. She could then make honest judgments about her actions.

The first four or five years are critical to establishing the framework from which the child will explore the world. The next ten years are almost as important. These are the years when children test out the surrounding environment. Using the patterns learned during the early years, children extend themselves into the world in an attempt to discover their place in that world.

A loving, secure environment is essential during this stage of development. The parent needs to allow the child to develop slowly, in their own way, according to their own patterns, but the parent must step in to protect the child in the face of disaster. Knowing when to step in and when to let the child work it out alone is the secret to good parenting.

Adolescence is the time of independence. It is often a messy, disjointed phase. The child must cast off that lifetime of watchful security, and strike out on their own. Often the combination of excitement and insecurity with regard to taking responsibility for one's own actions makes for some strident times. The rule for parents is *hands off*. The patterns of dealing with the environment are set. The experience of dealing with the world around them is learned. Be patient, and let this new person develop on their own.

Finally, they are no longer children, but adults. They are on their own to make of themselves what they will. If we look carefully, the markings of childhood are obvious and provide a connecting thread throughout their lives.

Obviously, aside from spending many of my coins on child rearing, I use a great many imbibing wine and a few other selected beverages. In fact, I sometimes receive a pittance of cash for writing such as this-- if it pertains to wine.

By now, I'm sure all of you see the connection.

Winemakers, cellar rats, and vineyardists are the extended family of fine wines. They nurture wines through their birth, childhood, and maturation into adulthood.

For wines, just as for children, the earliest stages are the most critical. Vineyard practices, vintage, and fermentation techniques lay an undeniable personality on any given wine. If vintage and fermentation produce a wine that is light and fruity, no amount of guidance or pressure will successfully turn that wine into a powerful, tannic monster. In a hot vintage with very ripe fruit and high sugars and no room in the winery to work with the juice, the wine will probably be big, alcoholic and rough, no matter how you try to soften it.

The secret lies in determining the possibilities, the distinct personalities, and then providing the technique and security of environment to allow them to develop to their fullest. The mistake is to try and force them to become something they're not. For this reason, each vintage as well as each variety must be treated differently, with respect for their individual characteristics.

The second stage of wine development involves storage, blending and barrel aging. Here, the winemakers and cellar rats must be diligent to watch for disasters. Bacteria, yeasts, oxygen, leaking valves, dirty hoses and careless attitudes all represent dangers that can destroy a

8

delicate young wine. The wines need to develop on their own, but we must step in to protect them from outside dangers.

Wine adolescence is bottling. The changes can be drastic. That sweet, lovely, lively wine can become sullen, morose and dull. Remember, *hands off*. By this time it's out of your hands. The parenting is done. Sit back, ride it out, and see what develops. If you've done your job by creating a warm, healthy environment, if you've protected the babies from disaster and allowed them to develop in their own way, then you have nothing to do but take joy in the fascinating adults they are about to become.

REJECTION

I was sipping ice-cold beer with Chuy. We sat in the hot sun watching my garden grow. Our tans were developing admirably.

"*Practical Winery* rejected my last column," I said.

"Por que?" asked Chuy.

"They complained, because the column had nothing to do with wine."

"I don't see what that's got to do with anything. You're a private eye, not some pinche wine writer. You ought to dump that rag."

We drank some beer. Then Chuy said, "En otro mano, they let you print some pretty strange stuff, maybe stuff no one else would let you print."

Chuy always had a point.

In any case, rejection is a miserable experience. Imagine, after all these years, *Practical Winery* rejected a Jake Lorenzo column. Well, technically my daughter Jakelyn wrote it, but a Lorenzo by any other name is still a Lorenzo.

They rejected the column because nowhere in it did the subject of wine appear, a bogus criterion if I ever heard one. After all, newspaper columnists range far and wide for their topics. Columnists writing for *Playboy* aren't restricted to topics dealing with T and A. Don't forget Hugh Johnson used to write gardening books.

I've never viewed myself as a wine writer. I like to think of myself as, in the words of Charles McCabe, "a professional drinker." Hopefully, my columns share and reveal insights into the world around us. Being a professional drinker, many of these insights seem to have links to wine or the art of drinking itself, but that shouldn't exclude those insights that aren't directly linked to wine.

I've always looked at wine and winemaking as a metaphor for life. It seems obvious. We talk of wines as being young. We watch them grow to maturity. We worry about them getting over the hill. I don't know about you, but I sure as hell view my life that way.

I figure I'm in the growing-to-maturity phase, although Jakelyn's mother often says she'd appreciate it if I'd grow up, so I might still be in the young stage. I know I haven't peaked yet, because I survived the last Grant's Birthday party to the bitter end, got up early the next morning and cooked the horseneck clams we'd caught.

I know for certain I'm not over the hill, because my father showed up at the party, drank with the rest of us till the bitter end as well, and was right there with me cooking those clams. If he's not over the hill yet, then I know I've got a ways to go.

That's what the column was about. Not my dad. It was about getting horseneck clams and celebrating Grant's Birthday. Jakelyn wrote it. She shared and revealed considerable insights. I'm sorry you missed them. Maybe if you write *Practical Winery*, they'll send you a copy.

That column will probably come to be known as the lost Jake Lorenzo column. There used to be a different lost Jake Lorenzo column, but I found it and turned it in. They printed that one. This lost Jake Lorenzo column will probably become a collector's item and be worth a lot of money. Jakelyn and I could make so much money that we'll start a magazine of our own. If we do, we won't reject insightful columns, no matter what the topic.

Wishful thinking?

Maybe so, but no more farfetched than someone starting a winery, who actually thinks he will make money. From what I can see, magazines make even less money than wineries, but they haven't the talent to go so deeply in debt.

Isn't business fascinating? I'll tell you one last insightful thing about the wine business. At least if the whole thing goes into the toilet, you'll have a warehouse full of wine to drink away your sorrows. All a magazine editor will have is a drawerful of rejected columns, if they're smart enough to save them.

MY FAVORITE HOLIDAY
by
Jakelyn Lorenzo

First, I've got to say that being a senior in high school is not the easiest thing to be, but it sure must beat the hell out of being a high school English teacher.

I mean the world is in turmoil. Drugs and crime run rampant in America. The possible effects of deficit spending border on the catastrophic. El Nino may return to Northern California, but what do we get as an assignment? My Favorite Holiday.

Sounds a bit elementary, don't you think? What terrible chemically induced disasters produced so twisted a mind as to give this assignment to high school seniors? Do English teachers have any viable links with reality at all?

Not only that, but look at what America's crass commercialism has done to our holidays. Watch kids at Christmas time and you see unbridled greed. Thanksgiving is no longer a simple time to give thanks, it's turned into a paen to gluttony. My old favorite, Halloween, is filled with warped declarations like poisoned candy and razor-bladed apples punctuated by drunken adults stumbling from party to party dressed up like characters from a nightmare I once had after a bowl of menudo from Chuy's Burrito Palace. Washington and Lincoln have been reduced to excuses for white sales.

What's left?

Grant's Birthday, that's what's left.

I know about this obscure, unofficial holiday because of my Dad. My Dad is a bit unusual, not because he's a private eye, but because he's obsessed with tradition. He's pretty much left me alone to discover and confront life's choices in my own fashion, but whenever he sees an event that may be fraught with tradition, he cajoles me into participating.

That's why I was up at 5:30 a.m. on a crisp, cold April Saturday. Beside me was my Dad, and in back were Dr. Calamari and a world famous winemaker who prefers to remain anonymous.

We were on our way to Tomales Bay in search of the great Horseneck Clam, and if we were truly lucky, a genuine Gooey Duck. Here it was April 27th, the official day of celebration for Grant's Birthday and we had a minus tide in a month that had an "R" in it. This bizarre coincidence was not lost on those of us in the car. It was, as my dad put it, an event that made the occurrence of Haley's comet pale in the sky like a champagne cork from a bottle of Cold Duck. (I realize this simile is a little oblique, but Dad had already done two shots of Hornitos in honor of the great General.)

We got to Lawson's Landing about 6:15 a.m. We got the boat in the water pretty fast considering that Dad spent all his time packing snacks and tequila bottles, while Dr. Calamari kept banging this device (that resembled an over-grown wine-powered pacemaker) on a cabernet bottle. I guess world famous winemakers are good for something, if you get them early enough on Grant's Birthday, and you need to get a boat in the water.

We were out on Hog Island by 6:30. The digging was easy and my dad's long arms made harvesting simple. Dr. Calamari was wandering around pouring cabernet into his device and holding it low to the sand. He didn't dig one clam. About an hour and a half later, we had limited out. We had two buckets full of what has to be the most obscene food in nature. At just this moment,

Dr. Calamari started jumping up and down and yelling things in Italian. As best I could make out, his wine-powered Gooey Duck finder had located a Gooey Duck.

Dad and the world famous winemaker hustled over there and started digging. It was a slow process. Took over two hours. The hole was over four feet deep. The walls were kept from caving in with the assistance of a hollowed out trashcan. Clammers came from all around to watch. Dad passed around the Hornitos bottle. When they finally got that Gooey Duck up, everybody cheered and sang a chorus of "For He's a Jolly Good Fellow." It was sweet to see. My dad had this great look on his face.

The ride home was joyous and loud. We put the clams into water with corn meal for later. Then we went over to the world famous winemaker's house for the Grant's Birthday celebration.

A Grant's Birthday Party is difficult to describe. People come and go throughout the night and well into the next morning. I make big bucks driving people home when they realize they're smashed. My dad pays me $5.00 an hour, and the tips are pretty good.

I enjoy watching all these old folks dancing and laughing and getting drunk. Usually, most old folks are tense and unsmiling. Grant's Birthday makes them loose.

The next afternoon, we cooked up those clams and the Gooey Duck, and had a feast for all the people who crashed at our house after the party. The food was pretty good. The company was fine, in spite of their hangovers.

I have been captivated by the spirit of the whole thing, and that's why Grant's Birthday is my favorite holiday.

A GOOD BOOK

Close your eyes. Conjure up an image of a private eye. What do you see?

A sad-faced man with a twinkle in his eye. Someone with that knowing Humphrey Bogart-Robert Mitchum tired grace and vulnerability. A simple, honest sort who doesn't mind mixing it up with the tough guys. A romantic, who's always in love, but never quite gets the girl.

Forget it. That's not the way it is at all.

Private investigators are more often nice guys just trying to get by. Most of our work is tedious and rarely life-threatening. Much of it is mundane. To supplement our income, we often work as repossessors, process servers, security cops, and bodyguards.

We spend a great deal of time sitting and waiting. We know how to use libraries. We are accustomed to scanning microfilm, digging through old newspaper files and dealing with bureaucrats to get access to obscure public records.

We get paid by the hour, or the day. Sitting and waiting has its rewards. The trick is to fill the hours. Personally, Jake Lorenzo likes to read, mostly fiction.

I read lots of detective novels for laughs, especially on planes, but I prefer off-the-wall modern fiction or just out-of-the-mainstream classics. My favorite all time book is *Catch 22*, for very Jake Lorenzian reasons. I read it at least once a year, just to reassure myself all is askew with the world.

For those of you who know how to read, here's a list of some of my finds: *Bless Me Ultima* by Rudolfo Anaya, the classic in Chicano literature; *Soul Catcher* by

Frank Hebert, famous for *Dune,* but insightful about Indian life; *Population 1920* by Jim Thompson, classic off-the-wall; almost anything by Harry Crews; early works by Don DeLilo and Robert Coover; all of John Steinbeck; most of John Irving, Celine, Hemingway, Thomas Berger and Elmore Leonard. Recently, I reread the *Autobiography of Malcolm X* by Alex Haley. It's incredibly good. Everyone must read *The Color Purple* by Alice Walker for its simple beauty and passion.

I bring this up for several reasons. First, in addition to being a private investigator, I fancy myself a wine columnist. After all, I've been writing these wine columns for 9 years now. I know it's egotistical, but I like to think I'm one of the best wine columnists in the business. I mean, who would you rather read, Bob Balzar? Terry Robards? Norm Roby?

Jerry Mead is famous for his industry gossip, but he'll be blown away when my first novel hits the bookstands. The title is *Kiss Off.* The plot involves a blackmail ring that dresses up underage girls to look older than they really are, and then takes them to wine tastings where they seduce winemakers, take photos of them in compromising positions, and blackmail them. The hero, based on yours truly, breaks up the ring by disguising himself as a flasher to gain acceptance into the inner circle of the blackmail ring. Eat your heart out, Jerry.

And Tony Blue, who has never recovered from that night he OD'd on sauternes and fell asleep reading *The Book of Lists* is going to plotz when he sees my new cookbook, *In The Kitchen With Jake Lorenzo.*

Here are a few sample recipes.
STEAK JAKE
3 T scallions
3 T chives
3 T parsley

1 T Worcestershire sauce
3 T olive oil
4 filet steaks
1/4 cup Hornitos tequila
Saute first four ingredients in 1 T olive oil. Set aside. Saute steaks in remaining oil in HOT pan. Top each steak with some scallion mixture. Flame with warmed tequila. Spoon pan juices over steaks and serve.

TOMATOES A LA NICKI
6 tomatoes
1 cup fresh basil
1/3 cup olive oil
1/2 cup Parmesan cheese
Peel and core tomatoes. Turn upside down and salt. Puree other ingredients. Stuff puree into tomatoes and chill.

JAKE'S JUNKIE DROPS
2 egg whites
1 tsp. vanilla
1/8 tsp cream of tartar
1/8 tsp salt
2/3 cup sugar
1 pkg (12 oz.) chocolate chips
Beat the egg whites until soft peaks form. Add vanilla, cream of tartar and salt. Gradually add sugar, beating until whites are stiff. Fold in chocolate chips. Grease a cookie sheet lined with wax paper. Drop the cookies onto the cookie sheet and bake at 300 F for 20-25 minutes.

See, Tony, I managed to get two lists into one column.

I know this is rambling, but I hope it's been interesting. Cook up these recipes, wash them down with some great California wines and then read yourself to sleep with a good book.

In the meantime, Jake Lorenzo will probably be sitting in a cold car, listening to his tapes, sipping a little Hornitos, waiting for something to happen, but at least I'll be getting paid.

THE BIG PICTURE

We were celebrating Paraquat's release from jail. Liz dipped chips into Chuy's hot sauce and kept an eye on their baby, Teddy "Bear" Parducci, as he crawled around on the floor.

Chuy, standing on a step stool, pounded a nail into the wall above the cash register. "Cuidado Bear, no mata las cucurachas. They add to the ambiance."

Bear drooled over a chip and ignored Chuy.

Paraquat talked about his next project. "It's gonna be great, Jake. We're calling it the American Odyssey. Liz and Bear and I are leaving next week. The Odyssey takes us through 12 states and we'll be doing 16 paintings.

"Each painting will reflect the surroundings. Lots of greens in the rain forests of Washington. Browns and reds in the Painted Desert. I've even worked out a technique that incorporates glitter for Las Vegas."

"We figure it will take three months," said Liz. "We should be back in time to celebrate Bear's first birthday."

I nodded, thinking to myself that if they got caught at half the painting sites and got 30 days for each one, they would be lucky to get back for Bear's second birthday.

Chuy hung up the framed poster I'd brought him for Christmas and stepped back to look. We all looked up at the picture of Marcelo Hernandez sitting proudly on his tractor. "Como se dice vino en Baja Sonoma? I love it, Jake."

"It's great," said Liz.

Bear burped.

I poured another glass of zinfandel, *RED* zinfandel. "I got that poster in the mail along with a note from the winery that said it was released in recognition of and thanks to the people who bring in the harvest.

"When I called the winery to tell them how much I liked it, Jim McCullough told me he sent out more than three dozen of them to various wine writers and industry publications. I was the only one to respond or mention the poster at all."

"Pinche press," said Chuy. "They don't know what's news. This is the first time I ever seen a winery mention that my people had anything to do with making wine. This ain't just news, this is a breakthrough."

Paraquat got up. "We've got to be going. Liz's folks are expecting us." He scooped Bear into his arms and walked to the poster. He stared at Marcelo for a long while. Softly, he said. "Look at it, Bear. It's part of the Big Picture."

Liz hugged them both, and they left.

"Que dicen sus amigos, Jake? What the hell's the Big Picture?"

I got up from my stool, and went to the poster. I looked at it hard, then I smiled. "It's something that Paraquat taught me about his freeway paintings. The Big Picture is the heart and soul of the artist. When the artist has done his job right, the finished work is like a tunnel that illuminates the spirit of the moment."

"So, how do you know if something is part of the Big Picture or not?"

"That's easy," I said. "If something is truly part of the Big Picture, it makes you act. It makes you take some sort of action."

A couple of years ago, in these pages, I wrote that the industry should provide technical winemaking and viticultural information in Spanish to facilitate the education and development of Spanish-speaking members of the industry.

It is time to do so. Chuy, myself, and the California Growers Foundation are calling for funding for the Marcelo Hernandez Honorary Chair for bilingual information. We anticipate making a series of video tapes that will be made available to anyone in the wine industry. We will also produce a series of bilingual pamphlets.

These tapes and pamphlets will cover modern viticultural practices with emphasis on vineyard theory, growth and pests. They will also explain basic enology techniques, use of equipment and varietal information. Emphasis will be placed on the connection between the vine and wine from grape to glass.

The funds should come from wineries based on Jake Lorenzo's Modest Proposal (JLMP). The JLMP says that the next time a wine writer or a sales rep from some publication comes over for a free lunch, forget about going to some fancy restaurant. Instead, start the coals, heat some tortillas and fire up some carne asada. Toss in some killer hot sauce, and while that wine writer or sales rep tries to extinguish his burning taste buds, explain the facts of life in the vineyard to him.

Let him know that were it not for Hispanic workers, there would be *no* California wine industry. Tell him that these dedicated, hard working people have earned the right to the kind of information that will allow them to advance into positions of responsibility in the winemaking side of the industry.

Then take all of the money you've saved on the lunch and earmark it for the Marcelo Hernandez Honorary Chair. It will make you feel good. Give you something to celebrate. And if you're going to celebrate, what better to drink than some fine vino de California?

The paperwork to set up the fund is in motion. Please contact *Practical Winery* for information on where to send funds, or watch for details in this space in future issues.

(Jake's note: After a full year, we had received donations from Matanzas Creek, Hanzell and The Cutler Cellar. Those were the only wineries to respond. I returned the checks with a thank you, and temporarily gave up on my plans to provide bilingual information to the people who need it.)

ESCARGOT

To understand, we must go back to a warm summer evening in 1991. Jakelyn's mother and I were at the Berthoud's for our second annual "Escargot Feed."

The Escargot Feed is a thing of beauty and gluttony. The four of us sit at the Berthoud's delightful table. Each of us has a metal dish with six divots. Each divot is filled with a plump escargot swimming in garlic, parsley and butter sauce. We use those wonderful escargot pincers, and slowly eat the snails, sopping up the sauce with delicious homemade bread, and washing everything down with Claude's exquisite zinfandels.

Upon finishing the first round, Ann takes the plates into the kitchen and fills them with more escargot. We eat, half-dozen batch by half-dozen batch, until we are too weary with the richness of it all to continue. To cleanse the palate, a crisp green salad appears on the table. We finish with a light, freshly baked fruit tart that Ann seems to whip up at a moment's notice.

Jakelyn's mother and I go home, have a small glass of vintage port, and then go to bed.

I cannot sleep. The wine, the company, and the escargot combine to make a rich, heady mixture that has my mind racing. Full blown, a poster idea explodes in my brain. I get up from bed and make notes.

*   *   *

A few weeks later, we photographed a poster for the Cutler Cellar. It's one of my favorites. It depicts a courtroom scene. A group of elderly, hostile judicial types question Lance Cutler. Lance is defended by his unflap-

24

pable attorney, played by Claude Berthoud. The caption reads, " Are you now or have you ever drunk a bottle of wine?" "Absolutely," is the reply, "and I'll name names. The Cutler Cellar, where wine ain't no crime."

It was a great, fun-filled shoot with lots of energy, and good humor. After the shoot, Lance took the cast out for lunch at the Depot Hotel. It turned out to be one of those unforgettable afternoons. We had plenty of Mike Ghilarducci's great food and sucked down several bottles of fine wine. There was lots of laughter and good cheer, but one of Claude's lines became a sort of anthem for the afternoon. When we ordered the second bottle, early into the afternoon, Claude said, "Just two bottles a day, that's all we ask."

We roared. Every time we ordered another bottle we would say, "Just two bottles a day..." Pretty soon we could order a bottle of wine by simply saying, "Two."

We all went home, but you know Jake Lorenzo.

A few months later, 150 people were standing in front of Sonoma's City Hall shooting another poster. This time the poster was for Gundlach Bundschu Winery. All the people were holding bottles of wine. Our kids were there on their way to Little League or a dance recital. Zak (the photographer) was exhorting us in his overly exuberant way. People were shouting, "Two!" and waving their arms, and holding up two fingers. The caption for the poster read "Just two bottles a day... That's all we ask." It was great fun, and for several weeks thereafter, participants commented on how they had enjoyed the afternoon.

*   *   *

On October 9, 1992 the Sonoma Police Professionals Association issued a letter. This letter was sent to the

25

media, to City Hall and to various regulatory agencies. The letter said, in part:

"Should city property and young children be used to advertise the use of alcoholic beverages? We have seen a very disturbing poster, which does this very thing... Is this what we want our children to believe? Every day we see the tragic results of the abuses of drugs and alcohol in our city and our society. We support the educational efforts by schools and other agencies in an effort to inform our children of the horrible dangers of overindulgence in the consumption of alcohol...

...do we want our children to see us standing on the balcony of City Hall with jugs of wine, trying to tell everyone it is O.K. to overindulge?"

*   *   *

On October 16, 1992, Tim Tesconi wrote a front page story for *The Santa Rosa Press Democrat*. The story included a picture of the poster and reported that Donald Rowe, president of the Association, was asking that the posters be destroyed.

Representing the winery, Jim Bundschu said that he couldn't believe anyone would take the poster seriously. He said the poster was a joke. "Don't people read political cartoons in newspapers?"

*   *   *

Monday, October 19, 1992. Again the poster finds its way into the press, an a story in the *Wall Street Journal* that discusses the clash of wineries and government over health claims attributed to drinking wine. It quotes Jim Bundschu as saying that he believes the industry should

26

let the whole health issue fall by the wayside. Jim said, "To promote wine as healthful or detract from it because it's unhealthy misses the point. Wine is good for the human spirit and the soul... now let them try and take that away."

*   *   *

Tuesday, October 20, 1992. Sonoma's local paper, the *Index Tribune,* comes out with its front page story. Again, the poster is printed. Now, Association representatives claim that groups such as Mothers Against Drunk Driving and Social Advocates for Youth are applauding the Association's stand.

Bundschu requests that no one in the winery make any statements to the press except him. He says he doesn't want to make a big issue out of this, because it's a local brouhaha, and he thinks it's best not to split the community.

*   *   *

Jerry Mead and others are writing to support the winery. Supporters point out that less than 2% of drunk drivers nationally are arrested under the influence of wine, and the incidence of drunk driving in the wine country is no greater than in other areas of comparable population density.

Gundlach Bundschu receives a few very antagonistic calls, but the majority support the winery and "just don't understand all the fuss."

Saturday, October 23, 1992. This will likely go on for sometime, but Jake Lorenzo is on deadline and the time to speak is now.

My immediate reaction was to do a couple of new posters. One would depict the Bundschu clan dressed like 1920's style gangsters in front of a wall of their wine. In their arms are giant corkscrews, held like tommy guns. The caption reads, "Come and get us, coppers."

The other poster idea was to get the same 150 people in front of city hall. This time each would raise just a single middle digit, and the caption would read. "Okay, just one bottle a day."

*   *   *

In the meantime, Lance Cutler came by the house and gave me something he'd written. Knowing Lance, I was expecting a scathing diatribe. Instead, I was astonished by what he wrote. I'll share it with you:

"Sixteen years ago, my wife, our seven-year old daughter and I settled in Sonoma. We lived, and still live, in a small, 750-square foot cottage on almost two acres of land, with only our landlords for neighbors.

We raised our own vegetables, baked our own bread, and raised chickens, rabbits and quail for meat. We had fruit trees galore; cherries, plums, peaches, apples and figs. We made our own beer and wine.

I ran a small private school, got paid six hundred dollars a month, and every day thanked my lucky stars for allowing me to leave Los Angeles and discover Sonoma.

In those days, Sonoma was a sleepy little village. The only stop light in the whole valley was at Fifth Street West, by the Safeway, (which used to be Hanns Kornell's winery.) The ducks pretty much ran the plaza, much to the delight of our daughter. Tourists were rare sightings, like red-tail hawks in the fall.

People were incredibly friendly, in that way unique to small towns. Shopping at the French Bakery or Vella's for cheese and butter was always warmed by laughter and local gossip.

We were blessed.

In 1978, I went to work for Gundlach Bundschu Winery, and in three short years, I became winemaker. Towle and Mary Bundschu were delightful people, and they graciously welcomed me and my family into their lives.

In those days, we produced 7,000 cases, operated on a shoestring, and had nothing but third-hand equipment. We worked 70-80 hours a week and loved it. In the summer, our children would laugh and giggle as they slapped labels on cases and helped on the bottling line. During harvest, our kids would come to the vineyards so they could drive the tractors. Afterwards, our families would sit down to simple, hearty meals. We'd drink the wine we had made with our own hands: men, women and children; Hispanic and gringo. Our children were always with us.

We were doubly blessed.

Jim Bundschu and I became best friends. We worked hard together and were proud of what we produced. As proud as we were of our wines, we took more pride in the way we ran our business. Ours was a family business, and the people who worked for us were part of that family. We were sometimes wild and crazy and always fun-loving. We worked as hard as anyone could, and that combination of hard-working, fun-loving dedication is what put a special magic into those bottles of Gundlach Bundschu wine.

We had discovered a secret, and we wanted to share it with the whole world. We wanted to show everyone what fun there was in work, in creating. We wanted to let people see the special magic created when a diverse group of people worked together to achieve a common goal.

Quite simply, more than sharing our wine, we wanted to share the joy that went into the making of it.

Granted, joy is a tough thing to convey, but we tried in our own unique way. We invented *Fortune Corks*, corks with fortunes printed on them. We created a series of posters, where we humorously depicted our lives in the wine business. We constructed a wall and painted a mural over 100 feet long depicting the contribution of Hispanic workers to the wine industry. And of course, we donned our masks and capes to raid the Napa Valley Wine Train.

I don't know how successful we've been at sharing our joy, but there is no doubt that the Sonoma secret is out. Sonoma's population has exploded. Stop lights are on every corner. Tourists clog our square, day and night. They fill our shops, restaurants and hotels. They visit our wineries, look at the beauty of our valley, and often decide to become locals themselves.

Sonoma is still a wonderful place to live, but make no mistake, it is changing. People are moving here in droves, and have been for years. This rapid growth erodes our small town spirit, and jeopardizes the very lifestyle we seek to preserve and enjoy.

The only things linking Sonoma to her sweet, small town past, are the vineyards dotting the valley. It's not the business generated by the wine industry that makes Sonoma special. It's the cyclical, agricultural family life style afforded us by the growing of grapes and the making of wine.

For those of us in the wine business, wine is our life. Our lives proceed one vintage at a time.

Most of our children are conceived shortly after harvest, when we reacquaint ourselves with our spouses.

You can tell when our children were born by looking in our wine cellars. We mark their births by harvest conditions: Jack was born in '89, the vintage from hell; Jill was born in '85, a perfect growing season. We track the important events in their lives through the growing season: he started school when we had that incredible frost in '90; she starred in the school play when we had early bud break in '87.

For those of us who make wine, it is impossible to separate our lives from our produce, because when we drink the wine we make, it starts memories of our very lives flowing in our veins.

When people tell me that the wine at my table is a sure sign that I'm an alcoholic, I laugh and go about my business.

When the government tells me that I've got to put warning labels on my wine, I comply and counter with a poster.

But when my children come home from school to report their teacher says wine is a drug like cocaine or heroin, then I am righteous in my indignation, because the very survival of my family is at stake.

And when the police say that I am corrupting children and must destroy a poster that clearly exudes heartfelt joy, I say this used to be America, and I will defend myself if I must.

For the past several years, all of us who enjoy wine have been under attack. We conceived the poster as a humorous way of defending ourselves, and reminding all of us how much we love wine and the life it provides each and every one of us.

I sincerely apologize to anyone who participated in this project for any pain or embarrassment caused by the reaction to this poster, but if doubts cross your mind, for even a second, just look at the poster and think back to that day.

You will smile at the excitement of your children, and grin at the poses of your dogs. You'll enjoy seeing your friends and neighbors, and you'll remember the sense of fun and community we shared. Finally, you'll laugh at the thought that anyone could take this seriously.

Sonoma was the birthplace of wine in California. The vineyards around us are our last line of defense against runaway growth. Winemaking stands at the heart of the Sonoma lifestyle and economy. The Sonoma way of life is a gift, directly attributable to winemaking and grape growing. It is a gift those of us in the industry gladly share with everyone.

All we ask is that they understand from whence the gift comes. It is no less than our very lives and the lives of our children. That's the magic in the bottle. That's the treasure we hope to share."

*   *   *

You can always count on the people who make wine to get to the heart of the matter, especially when the matter is wine.

I'll tell you what gets to Jake Lorenzo in all of this. The sentiment conveyed in Lance's article is exactly at the center of the wine industry. It's a family thing. Everyone in the wine industry should relate to that sentiment, or they should get out of the business.

What's frightening is how quickly people run for cover.

The Sonoma Police Professionals Association is not the Supreme Court. It is just a group of people who voiced some concerns about alcohol abuse. They have a right to

32

their opinion. In this particular case, I think their concern is misplaced.

We don't need to make a big hullabaloo about the police. We don't need to denigrate their fears about alcohol.

We do, however need to tell them our views. We need to explain, as Lance has done so eloquently, that there is a joyous, responsible way to view wine and alcohol. We need to explain that wine can be a good thing, that it can build a stronger sense of family, and that it can build a stronger sense of community. We need to tell them that wine is good for the human spirit and the soul.

This is what living in a democracy is about. We must speak up for our beliefs. We should not cringe when others disagree with us, nor should we fight back with antagonism. We must speak our minds and try to teach others what we know to be true.

PART II

Philosophic
Grumblings

POETS

Do you ever think about poets? Jake Lorenzo does. Poets somehow wear their emotions outside their skin, and the normal pummeling of day-to-day living becomes excruciating torture that forces them to scream their poems onto paper. Of course, nowadays no one reads poetry.

If Jake Lorenzo writes a poem and no one reads it, is Jake still a poet?

Alcohol is the beverage of choice among poets. Wear your emotions on the outside and you won't find a need for cocaine or uppers. No, rather a day full of beers, and a few bottles of wine to cool the burn, to anesthetize the pain.

Dylan Thomas was a poet, a great one say many. I know for a fact he was a great drinker. There are many who say that drink killed Dylan Thomas. Jake Lorenzo isn't one of them.

In detective novels and movies, the poor detective is always stuck in some intricate labyrinth of intrigue and cunning. He spends his time negotiating the corners and dead ends like a mouse in a maze, until he pops out the end and everything becomes clear.

Real life for the detective isn't like that at all. Usually, you begin knowing who's guilty. You know who's cheating on his wife. You know who embezzled the money. You know who stole the car. All the detective needs to do is be patient and get some proof.

That's why Jake Lorenzo is selective about what he reads and watches. It seems to me, that the most fascinating stories are about integrity. You know, a guy starts out with a dream. The dream rubs up against reality. The

35

guy compromises and slowly turns into the very thing he hates. Or he stays true to his dream and ends up crushed by life, but able to look at himself in the mirror.

If a man has a dream, but upon awakening can't remember, is it still a dream?

I guess it's the arrogance of detectives to think we always know what's going on. If we don't know now, we're sure to figure it out later. That's what accounts for the swagger in our voices.

Booze is still the beverage of choice among detectives. Know all the answers and you can afford to belly up to the bar and have a shot of whiskey (and the occasional tequila).

Jake Lorenzo is a detective, a great one say many. I know for a fact he's a great drinker. There are many who call Jake a wimp because he just drinks wine (and the occasional tequila), but don't say it to his face.

The wine industry was like a dream. That's what attracted me to it. It was idealistic young men and women deep in the dirt of hard work, drenched with the sweat of inspired labor and higher than kites on the possibilities of their magical product.

No one was too poor to risk the challenge, too tired to put in the hours, or too inexperienced to make the damn thing work.

Wine was the beverage of choice and the industry made it, drank it and reveled in the heady intoxicating wonder of building something from nothing. It was joyous and it was successful. It was people dedicated to making a better product each and every year by working harder each and every day. It was the best thing in American industry. Jake Lorenzo was delighted just to be close to it.

Success brought change. The dream rubbed up against reality. Maybe it wasn't enough to make good wine, to live in the glorious beauty of the wine country, to work long, hard hours producing something better each time out. Maybe we need a beautiful chateau, manicured gardens, even croquet courts.

Maybe it's not enough to throw some steaks on the fire and pound down about a case of young reds with the wine buyers from Chicago or New York or even Kansas City. Maybe it's not enough to let them share our joy at the honesty of our labor. Maybe we do have to fly them out, put them up, give them fancy meals, even put roses on their pillows.

All these maybes like some intricate labyrinth. All the mice running about in the maze.

For a while, I didn't get it. I couldn't see what was right in front of my eyes. I believed in the dream. Wine and its making was a joy that America would come to love, and the joy and the humor and the spontaneity and the irreverence would be embraced by the nation. Wine would be on every table, and every household would be the better for it.

Maybe the neo-drys are too powerful. Maybe capsules will be outlawed, sulfur will be banned and warning labels will obscure even the boldest label. Maybe sin taxes and initiatives will overburden small wineries until corporate wineries and foreign investors buy them out and acquire their vineyards. Maybe wine won't be the best thing in American industry. Instead, wine will be just another industry in America.

To hell with the maybes. Will you be able to look at yourself in the mirror?

Practical Winery and Vineyards says Jake Lorenzo isn't funny anymore, that's why they won't print some of my columns. I say a dream is dying and like a poet my words scream onto paper.

Dylan Thomas said, "Rage, rage, rage against the taking of a vision."

Jake Lorenzo says, "Take a look in the mirror."

When Jake looks in the mirror, his eyes are going to be bloodshot, because if he doesn't drink that second bottle, who will?

SHEEP

Don Novello wrote a book when he wasn't being Father Guido Sarducci. Entitled *Blade*, the book is a typical high school annual, purportedly from Schellville High School. (Schellville is the low-rent district southwest of Carneros.) Don's book is unique in that every student, teacher and administrator is a sheep.

Don's sheep are individuals. Each has a distinct personality, from the goofy Larry "Bummer" Brannon to vivacious Sandy Grubb to the sexy Taggart twins. Don's sheep have varied interests from the French Club to the Low Riders Club to the Sky Diving Club.

Alas, Don's book is fiction.

Sheep are not bright and they don't have distinct personalities. They wander aimlessly in flocks. Sheep don't have varied interests. They graze. No one considers it a compliment to be called, "A leader among sheep."

I know, you're asking, "Jake, what have you got against sheep?"

"Absolutely nothing," I answer, "in their proper place, which, as I see it, is on the table, roasted, preferably served with a big, chewy cabernet."

Speaking of tables, look what comes to ours.

America is the most bountiful country on this planet. Her abundant harvest provides a panoply of foods and flavors that staggers the imagination. Food producers in this nation have the capabilities to electrify our tastebuds with exquisite and exotic delights.

Yet the American marketeer (a leader among sheep) insists on reducing this cornucopia of flavors to a mish-mash of inoffensive goo designed to please the least of all distinguished palates. They spend millions of dollars in advertising to attract the sheep and entice them to spend

39

their hard-earned dollars on these compromised food-
stuffs.

So who's to blame? Not the marketeer. He's just
out to make a few bucks, to generate some business, to
provide a few jobs. Surely not the sheep. Their job is to
graze and maybe get a haircut once a year so we can have
some fancy clothes. No, they're not to blame.

In fact, this column has nothing to do with blame,
nothing at all. This column's about sheep, remember?

I'll tell you what I like about sheep. They don't do
drugs. That's right, when was the last time you saw a
sheep with dilated pupils from toking on one too many a
joint? Ever see a sheep with a runny nose from too much
cocaine? I'd be willing to bet there's never been a sheep
voluntarily hooked on heroin.

People, on the other hand, are developing quite a
reputation for being addicts. We can get addicted to
anything from drugs to TV to religion to health food.
Addiction is so common a human condition, that nowadays certain addictions are fashionable.

Alas, this is fact.

Addicts think a little bit won't hurt them. It will.
Addicts always think they can quit. They can't. Addicts
always think they're in control. They're not. No one
wants to admit he's an addict.

"Jake," you cry, "what's wrong with wine coolers?"

"Jake, what have you got against white zinfandel?"

"Absolutely nothing," I answer again, "in their
proper place, which, as I see it, is in the grocery market, in
the bulk wine section, where the greedy American
marketeers have sold it to the sheep who think they need
to buy it."

The most pervasive American addiction today is
not drugs, or alcohol, or violence. Today's America is

addicted to mediocrity. It affects everyone and has permeated every thread of our American fiber.

Like all addictions, mediocrity is insidious. No one sets out to be mediocre. On the contrary, we start with the highest of intentions.

You know, maybe you're going to produce the finest, most intense red wine mankind has ever had the pleasure of sampling.

And you do it. You've produced the world's greatest red wine, but it doesn't sell. You start to doubt yourself. Could you be wrong? No, certainly not. So like the other addicts you put the blame for your addiction on outside forces. You know, the reviewers think the alcohol's too high, the restaurateurs think the tannin's a bit harsh, the retailer thinks the label's too drab. All of which leads you to that first (how shall we say it?) compromise.

You know, just a little can't hurt. You'll just pick the grapes a little sooner, fine the wine a little heavier, do the packaging a little slicker. But just to improve the cash flow a little so you can go back to your goal of making, uh, really good...uh good tasting...uh wine.

Remember, addicts, the first one's free. Just a little bit can't hurt. You're not selling out, just compromising a little. The critics still don't like your wine. It lacks character, they say, but to hell with the critics. It's starting to sell, and you can get some lousy zinfandel cheap, and blush wines are in, so you'll just make what the sheep want, and you'll be rich, which is almost as good as making great red wine. At least you'll be able to buy it if someone else makes it.

I don't blame you. This is not about blame. It's not about sheep anymore, either.

Jake Lorenzo wants to thank those of you who resist. Bless you for resisting the compromise. Power to you for believing in your convictions and for pursuing your dreams. We're not all sheep, and while I can't guarantee it, I think there's enough of us out here to support you and keep you going.

And God bless those who refuse to be sheep, who seek out and support the committed, dedicated producers of the world.

Anyone can be a hero. Anyone can resist. No less a star than Bill Cosby said, "I don't know the key to success, but the key to failure is trying to please everybody."

DEAR JOHN

Dear John:

The moon is grinning tonight. A sly grin. The night is balmy. I'm working on an interesting case. I have lots of time to think, to philosophize. Since you're the only person I know who claims to be a philosopher, I'm addressing these ruminations to you.

Jake Lorenzo's philosophy comes directly from long hours spent observing ants. There are always ants. Ants have a long noble history. Industrious buggers. Working, hauling, always on the move.

Everyone has watched ants. We've seen the long trains of two-way traffic like cars on a freeway. We've all seen the intricate tunnels and pathways of an ant farm. We've all watched an ant struggle with a load much bigger and heavier than he was.

And each of us, in a fit of anger or depression or plain mean-spiritedness, has stood with a hose blasting hundreds of ants to oblivion like so many Egyptian soldiers in the Red Sea.

So, John, I sit here under the grinning moon thinking there are levels. Ants are one level. They live in a world, work hard, raise a family, but occasionally they are suddenly, horribly, tragically destroyed by floods, poisons or big feet.

Ants have a saying for these catastrophes. Ants say, "Fate does what it wants, ants have to keep on marching."

Here John, we have a philosophy to live by. After all, man is just another level. We live in a world, work hard, raise our families and occasionally are suddenly,

43

horribly, tragically destroyed by floods, cancers or car crashes.

Doesn't it make you think, John? Who's squirting the damn hose? Who is this Fate?

I can tell you, John, it makes me think. It surely does.

Speaking of getting hosed, let's look at this last harvest. What a year. CRUSH starts and never stops. Everything is ripe at once. Pickers can't keep up. Wineries are jammed. The world's supply of tartaric acid is at an all-time low. And the moon is grinning. Have I mentioned that, John?

I watched this harvest. I marveled at the majestic, sweeping power of Mother Nature. I sat stunned by the avalanche of this harvest.

But I saw raw courage and bravery in the face of such carnage. I saw people without sleep, rest, or strength summon nerves to work more. Mother Nature can do what she wants. Cellar rats have to keep on working.

In light of the unprecedented weirdness of this harvest, and in light of the tremendous burden it placed directly on the backs of cellar workers everywhere, I find it ludicrous when I hear the annual mouthings of a few who continue to bray, "It's the best year ever."

It was not the best year ever, but like every other year, it was different from all the others. In its own way, 1984 will create its own unique wines, and like newborn children they will grow to have lives of their own.

And John, the moon is grinning. I think it knows something.

> Love,
> Jake

WINE WRITERS

The day-to-day reality of a private eye is mundane. We are rarely involved in high-speed chases, bloody shoot outs, or continual physical abuse. Seldom are our clients gorgeous and, alas, even more seldom do they drag us hot and lathered to their beds.

We are, however, often exposed to some of the true scum of the earth, vermin generated out of greed who prey on the weak and the guilty. I have, in my time, rubbed up against some pretty unsavory characters.

But as mean spirited as these people can be, there's a code, an underlying honesty inherent in their actions. The drug addict steals to support his habit, not out of spite for his victims. The blackmailer operates out of greed without any other pretense.

Don't get me wrong, Jake Lorenzo does not condone blackmail or robbery. I have no romantic notions about crooks and criminals, but I do understand and respect them as adversaries. In my line of work, you either do that or you wind up in some emergency room trying to eat through a tube.

Having read all this, you may find it laughable when I say for pure, unfettered slime you can't do much better than your average, run-of-the-mill wine writer.

I'm not talking about guys like Gerald Asher who, at his best, writes with a heartfelt lyricism that often brings tears to my eyes. Bob Thompson keeps searching for those perfect turns of phrase that he drops like pearls while he staunchly goes on educating the public to unfashionable pleasures in the world of wine. Rod Smith, who comes from another planet, writes about wine with great love, but from such a unique perspective that I always finish stunned by the wonder of it.

These people are writers. We see in their work attempts to understand the world around them. Wine is a metaphor through which they examine and reveal themselves.

But on the other end of the spectrum are the nameless scum who prey on the wine business and, like so many leeches, suck its life blood.

People who insist on paid advertising in exchange for favorable reviews. People who save up petty slights and insults until they can dish out crushing stories full of innuendo and misinformation. People who jump on bandwagons and support the chosen few while ignoring (and therefore often putting out of business) the non-trendy and unique. People full of self-importance dedicated to self-promotion. People on the dole, the take, the pad, the free lunch, the free trip and the free room. People who write from the wallet instead of the heart.

This whole thing is sickness. Each and every winery has been touched by it. None of this would happen if you didn't let it. Like any other slime, it can't survive in the bright, clear light of day. Bring it out in the open. You'll feel the better for it.

THE QUIXOTIC $1,000 CELLAR

I was sitting on my stool at Chuy's Burrito Palace. The coffee was hot. The tequila was Tres Generaciones, and we had just come from the 4th of July parade in Sonoma.

"That, amigo, is America. I love the parade in Sonoma," said Chuy. "Todos los ninos, their loco padres, los soldados, the flags, all the people drinking cerveza and Bloody Marys in the morning. It makes you proud to be a gringo."

"You're not a gringo, Chuy," I pointed out. "What's all this talk about pride?"

"Mira, Jake, tengo orgullo por que soy chicano. You don't have to be a stinking gringo to know about pride." Chuy's hand tightened on the neck of the tequila bottle.

"You're right about that, Chuy, but you are a little volatile on these holiday mornings, aren't you?" He laughed, caught in his fake tantrum, and poured us each another shot.

"It is a beautiful parade," I continued, "but what is it about America, where everything has to get bigger if we're to think it's getting better? There were over 1,000 people marching in this parade. Pretty soon, it won't be a small town parade. It'll be some major production, create its own deficit and they'll have to create some local tax to fund the damn thing."

"Es la verdad, amigo. In America, you gringos always want mas; more bigger, more expensive." Chuy sighed, "It is very sad. Gringos don't understand satisfecha. They're never satisfied with what they have.

They don't understand the secret is taking joy out of what you already have."

"Aha, another one of Chuy's secrets. Satisfecha. You mean to tell me that if some rich Japanese company came over here and offered you millions of dollars for franchise rights, there wouldn't be a proliferation of Chuy's Burrito Palaces across America. Given the opportunity, wouldn't you be the chicano McDonald's?"

"Jake, McDonalds is corporate fast food. Taco Bell is already the chicano McDonalds. Chuy's Burrito Palace is something else. If I franchised my business, then there would be another corporate fast food chain, but there would be no Chuy's Burrito Palace, and that would be a shame. Comprendas, amigo?"

And I did understand. As I walked to the cooler to get us two Bohemias, as I put my money on the counter, as Chuy rang up the sale, I understood everything.

*   *   *

Months ago, I had the misfortune to pick up an issue of *The Wine Spectator*. It touted their picks for the $10,000 wine cellar. Jake Lorenzo thought to himself, "Who the hell are these guys writing for?" I looked at those cellars, and I saw where Marvin Shanken said, "I only buy wines (for my cellar) that I believe will appreciate in value." This is why private eyes rarely carry loaded guns on their person.

While I was tearing through my closet, trying to find the bullets and get the gun loaded, another idea popped into my head. I didn't need to shoot anybody. I called Don Neel, my editor at *Practical Winery and Vineyards,* and told him I wanted to do a feature on $1,000 wine cellars (less than $3 per day). I told him I was going to get cellar rats from several different wineries to list their

48

$1,000 cellars. While I was at it, I thought I might take a few pokes at *The Wine Spectator* and other magazines of their ilk. To my surprise, Don said, "OK."

I called several wineries, explained what I was going to do and why, and then I waited. Weeks passed. Then months. Only two wineries actually sent me lists for their $1,000 cellars.

When I got back in touch with the other wineries, they hemmed and hawed, but eventually they mentioned that maybe it wouldn't be in their best interests to poke fun at so illustrious a publication as *The Wine Spectator*.

It doesn't happen easily, but Jake Lorenzo was shocked. I spent a great part of the next two months mulling over all the implications, but I couldn't pull it together. Not until the 4th of July in Chuy's Burrito Palace.

*   *   *

On July 5th, Jake Lorenzo went and found a windmill. On a bright blue windswept afternoon he climbed that windmill and affixed a lightning rod. Then he went to the bank, drew out a hefty sum of money, and went to vote.

Jake Lorenzo lives in America. America is a democracy. That means Jake Lorenzo can make choices. It is Jake's responsibility to learn about important topics, so he can make informed choices.

America's economic system is capitalistic. It holds that individuals can own land, factories and other means of production to produce goods and services to compete with one another in a free market for profit.

Jake Lorenzo is not a politician or an economist, but I am a consumer and a citizen. I have devised a system that combines politics and economics, democracy and capitalism. It is deceptively simple. I call it voting with your dollars.

The system works like this: Everytime you spend money, whether it's for food, clothing, consumer goods or services, you are deciding which businesses will survive and which shall fail. You are, in fact, making choices, and these choices, over time, will drastically alter your future way of life.

Spending money in America (and more and more throughout the world) is a political act. It provides a unique and dramatic impact especially at a local level. Sadly most consumers are unaware of this very real political power. They spend their dollars mindlessly and remain ignorant as to how they are changing the life around them.

Let's use buying a bottle of wine as an example. You are a consumer. You enjoy drinking wine. You go to the store where hundreds upon hundreds of bottles from hundreds upon hundreds of producers await. You make your choices, then you go to the cash register and vote with your dollars.

When you buy wine, you vote to drink.

You vote against prohibition. You vote to retain the right to use your own judgment with regard to alcohol instead of suffering the imposition of someone else's idea of what is correct.

The varieties of wine that you purchase will eventually determine which grapes are planted and which are ripped out. The wineries that you support stay in business, grow and prosper. The wineries that you don't support struggle and go broke.

You as a wine consumer have a very real impact on what the wine business of the future will look like. Think wines are too expensive? Stop buying them and start buying cheaper ones.

Bored with living in a chardonnay-cabernet world? Stop buying them. Go to pinot, merlot, gewurz. Hell, try a riesling again.

Tired of the glistening show palaces of stainless steel excess that have become our wineries? Stop visiting. Seek out the few remaining rustic, charming, workplaces that are left.

Hate standing in the supermarket trying to figure out which of the thousands of wines to buy? Get thee to a wine shop and talk to a real person who loves wine and knows the difference between wine and frozen peas.

Since every time you go shopping, you are voting, it's critical that you be informed. First and foremost, you want to get good value for your hard earned dollars. Second, and almost as important, you want to be sure you are voting for things you believe in.

Where are you going to get that all important information?

You aren't going to get it from Robert Parker or Marvin Shanken. Lists of wines, scores and ratings tell us very little about the true quality of a wine, and they tell us absolutely nothing about the philosophy or practices of the maker of that wine.

Personally, I am uncomfortable getting my wine information from publications that take advertising from wineries. The line between hospitality and payoff is a fine one. The hard economic times ahead blur that line and inevitably lead to crossing over it. The mere fact that there is an underground murmur throughout the industry that wonders if ratings are bought, should be enough to cause wineries to stop purchasing those ads.

Jake Lorenzo chooses to get his wine information from people who love wine and are awed by the magic of it. I want my information from people who buy and drink wine for the joy it brings to our lives. I want to hear from people who work in the fields and who struggle in cold damp cellars. I want to hear from people who make their livelihoods in the wine business.

I don't need to know which wines some expert thinks will appreciate in value. I don't need to know which swells attended which auction or which lot of wine sold for the most ridiculous amount of money.

Tell me who is ecologically conscious in the vineyard. Tell me who respects their workers and pays them a fair wage. Who's fun and who's pretentious? Who makes their living from wine and who uses it to adorn their lifestyle? Tell me what I need to know so I can use my dollars to support those things that are important to me. Put the real information out there and let the public decide who succeeds and who fails.

*   *   *

So, you've got some money in your pocket and you're itchin' to vote. Here's some advice.

Kenwood Vineyards is a family run business. The Lee brothers and brother-in-law John Sheela have directed things since the early 70's. They were one of the first to go with an artist label in California. They have a very experienced and wild cellar crew, many of whom are settling down as they have families. The legendary Chuy Ordaz runs the vineyard crew. They initiated bilingual classes to help workers deal with government immigration laws. One of the first to have a profit sharing plan. They like Jack London. One of only two wineries to turn in a $1,000 cellar.

The Kenwood Vineyards
$1,000 Cellar
Note: Buy by the case. Discount may be 20% Open a red from a particular case once a year until it reaches

52

perfection, or some reasonable facsimile thereof, then finish the case. For whites, open a bottle every few months, unless it's expected to be a long ager.

List:

1 bottle Conmemorativo Tequila	$20
(por la fiesta)	
1 bottle Hennessy	$24
(for educational purposes: to taste French oak)	
1 bottle Old Grand Dad	$13
(to taste American oak)	
1 case 1986 Caymus "Napa Valley"	$240
Cabernet Sauvignon	
1 case 1985 Laurel Glen	$240
Cabernet Sauvignon	
1/2 case 1988 Kenwood "Beltane Ranch"	$84
Chardonnay	
1/2 case 1988 Kistler "Durrell Ranch"	$96
Chardonnay	
1 case Gundlach Bundschu Merlot	$180
(pick a year)	
1 case 1990 Kenwood Sauvignon Blanc	$108
(It will be a good one!)	
1/2 case 1987 Kenwood Zinfandel	$66
1/4 case 1987 Haywood Zinfandel	$36
1/4 case Gundlach Bundschu Zinfandel	$30
(pick a year)	

Gundlach Bundschu Winery will have its 133rd consecutive harvest in 1991. They make 16 different wines each year. Their wild, crazy sense of humor infiltrates their famous poster series, Time for Wine hats, fortune corks, radio commercials and general demeanor. Marcelo Hernandez has run the vineyards for more than 20 years. They have a 120 feet long mural honoring Hispanic workers in the wine industry. Regularly take front line positions supporting wine and agriculture in Sonoma

Valley. Great Tequila drinkers. Masterminds of the Sonoma Valley Wine Patrol's raid on the Napa Wine Train. One of only two wineries to turn in $1,000 cellar.

Gundlach Bundschu
Cellar Rations

Note: Maximum price limit of $25 per bottle

Whites:

1/2 case Sauza Tres Generaciones Tequila	$150
4 cases Mickey's Big Mouth Beer	$52
1 bottle Stoly Vodka	$20

Reds:

2 magnums Barefoot Bynum Cabernet Sauvignon	$12
2 cases Gundlach Bundschu Sonoma Red	$106
1/2 case Haywood Zinfandel 1986	$ 84
5 bottles Hanzell Pinot Noir 1986	$100
1 case Gundlach Bundschu 1988 Cab Franc	$132
6 bottles Gundlach Bundschu Vintage Reserve (1981-1986)	$144
1/2 bottle Chateau Latour 1984	N/A
(In keeping with our $25 per bottle price limit, we can't afford a full bottle, and we can't find it in splits.)	
1 case Guinness Stout	$28
1 bottle Bushmill's Black Bush	$20

Sparklers:

1 case Gloria Ferrer NV Brut	$126

Finally, Jake Lorenzo isn't a cellar crew, but I drink wine each and every day. I try to make every vote count.

Whites:
6 bottles   Sauza Tequila $100
       (Hornitos and Tres Generaciones)
3 bottles   Trimbach Gewurztraminer $27
       (I like Jean Trimbach. His is an old family.
       I gave him his first milkshake and his
       first shot of tequila.)
6 bottles   Gundlach Bundschu Gewurz $40
       (Gotta go with wild, crazy and irreverent)
Reds:
6 bottles   Hanzell Pinot Noir $100
       (One of my favorite wine makers. Soft spoken,
       but opinionated. Forges his own style in spite of
       current fads. High alcohol.)
6 bottles   Kenwood Jack London Pinot Noir $90
       (Great wine, good guys, and they honor a writer.)
3 bottles   Dehlinger Pinot Noir $45
       (Nice guy, honorable, generous with his
       employees. Family man with a family vineyard.)
1 case   Gundlach Bundschu Reds $140
       (Zin, Pinot, Merlot, Cab, Cab Franc, etc.
       consistently good, fair priced.)
1/2 case   Benziger Reds $70
       (Wild, fun loving, hard drinking family
       making good wine, and they have Charlie
       Tolbert working for them.)
3 bottles   Laurel Glen Cabernet Sauvignon $65
       (Patrick Campbell puts himself on the
       line politically. Great wines and has Ray
       Kaufman working for him.)
3 bottles   Preston Zinfandel $27
       (I like the wine, so I assume they are good people.)
1/2 case   Silverado Reds $70
       (Good quality and fair prices which makes
       them unique in Napa)

3 bottles	Frog's Leap Reds	$30

(Humor in Napa sticks out like a wart on the back of your hand.)

3 bottles	Tudal Cabernet Sauvignon	$40

(Wonderfully nice man. Gentleman farmer type with a real love of the land.)

3 bottles	Flora Springs Reds	$50

(Great people who define the word nice. Joyful spirits.)

The rest of the money I spread around to all those people I like, but will probably forget to mention. I mean you've got to get a bottle of Mondavi just because he led the fight against the prohibitionists. I have to buy from John Parducci and Jim Pedroncelli. A bottle of Qupe is a must simply to keep Bob in business until he comes to his senses and gives up on the Dodgers. You have to buy some Arrowood just to keep Alis in the industry, and they have Mike Berthoud working for them. It's a long list, but it enhances my enjoyment of each and every bottle when I remind myself that I'm keeping these wonderful people in business when I buy their wines.

*   *   *

It's any Sunday in Sonoma. Jakelyn's mother and I are making our rounds of the Plaza. We go into Sonoma French Bakery and wait in line with the tourists to get our bread. Then we go up to Vella's and wait in line with the tourists to get our cheese and butter. We go to Sonoma Sausage where we wait in line with the tourists to buy pate and sausage.

We don't like waiting in line, but we do enjoy the small town ambiance. We like talking to the familiar faces behind the counters. It's only after we have gone to all these small, independent business people that we go to the market and buy the rest of our groceries. We spend our time and fight the crowds, because in doing so we support a way of life we would like to live and if that's what it takes to vote for it, then you can count on Jake Lorenzo to be stuffing the ballot boxes.

*   *   *

Jake Lorenzo sits on the grass sipping a glass of red wine. He looks at the windmill and his eyes travel to the lightning rod affixed to the top. Jake knows the weather is soon to storm. He sips his wine, smiles and thinks to himself, "Don't start on me fellas. If we go to war, I'll cut you to shreds."

LADDERS

There is something about an election year that makes Jake Lorenzo ponder the difference between fantasy and reality.

Have you ever met people that are simply, outrageously funny? It's not that they are comical, it's just that they describe things in ways that never occurred to you and in ways that you find hilarious.

Or have you ever been faced with a problem, pondered it for hours or even days, only to have someone else come up and solve the problem with that instant insight that boggles the imagination?

I think this phenomenon is connected to ladders, mental ladders. Each person has a ladder in his mind and he climbs to a different rung on that ladder to view the world about him. When people surprise us with incisive insights that never would have occurred to us in a million years, they are simply giving their view from a particular rung on their mental ladder.

Put in a physical plane, the mental ladder phenomenon can best be explained by imagining two people, one tall and one short. They are both looking around a kitchen. The tall person has a fine view of the top of the refrigerator. He can see all the platters piled on top covered with dust. Believe me, the short person has no idea what the top of the refrigerator looks like, and unless he climbs up on a ladder, he isn't going to find out.

Since tall people spend all their time able to see the tops of refrigerators, while short people rarely go through the trouble of climbing up rungs on ladders to observe that particular view; tall people and short people have a different view of reality. Ask them to describe the world around them and you'll get two different descriptions.

A tall person's reality is a short person's fantasy.... and vice versa.

Think about it. George Bush and Bill Clinton live in the same world, but they see it in completely different ways. Not only do they envision different worlds, but for the life of them they can't understand how the other guy can be so screwed up.

Bush sees a gleaming new refrigerator. Clinton sees that the refrigerator is empty.

Until and unless people are operating from the same rung on their mental ladders, there is no way in hell to convince them to accept your own particular vision of reality, because to them it is pure fantasy.

This brings us to a phenomenon I call "Jake's Dilemma." What happens to the person whose fantasies *become* reality? If you imagine some great fantasy, and then go about making that fantasy happen so that it becomes reality for others, what the hell do you do?

Let's say you fancy yourself a writer, so you sit down once a month and write about whatever comes to mind. What if some weirdo with a magazine calls you each month demanding that you sell him whatever the hell you're writing about?

Let's say, for example, that you have a fertile imagination, a sarcastic sense of humor and a lot of free time on your hands. What if you organized a bunch of friends and hijacked a train and it made national news?

What if every time you come up with a funny idea about wine, some winemaker who says he's a friend of yours turns it into a poster? Pretty soon these posters are everywhere. People are calling you up asking you to do posters for them. People are sending you bribes to appear in your next poster.

59

If this kind of stuff is happening to you, then you have confronted "Jake's Dilemma." Of course, we may not be operating from the same mental rung here. Let Jake even up the ladders.

Let's say you like drinking wine. You're a little fed up with the rat race. You have a few bucks, so you decide to get in touch with nature, buy some land, plant a few vines, and make some vino. The years go by, and before you know it, you're in debt for $3 million. You spend all your time in suits at five course dinners and waiting to see buyers in closet offices in the back of liquor stores. Ain't that a fantasy run wild into reality?

Let's say your love of wine led you into the wine business. You got a job as cellar rat in some wonderful small winery operation. You worked your butt off, learned incredibly complex mechanics and science and laws of nature. You took pride in your work and pride in your product, but now find that you can't even afford to attend your own industry's awards night. You can't afford to attend your own wine auction. You can't afford to buy a bottle of your own wine in the fancy local restaurant. Ain't that fantasy turned into one son of a bitch reality?

What if you find your mind full of wildly bizarre ideas and you find yourself pursuing each and every one of them? When Jake Lorenzo's fantasies turn into reality he reverts to Jake's Law: *Go with the flow.* Any fantasy pursued is more fun than an idea left to raisin.

Here are the fantasies I'm working on. Look for them in a reality near you soon.

The Jake Lorenzo Wine Timer. The perfect thing for the wine snob who has everything. Insert the Jake Lorenzo Wine Timer into those bottles in your wine cellar, and it will let you know when your wine is ready to drink.

The Jake Lorenzo Wine IV. Why lose one of life's great pleasures just because you're hospitalized. The Jake Lorenzo Wine IV allows you to select your bottle and drip it too.

Retractable Vineyard Domes. Protect your chardonnay crop from the ravages of rain and mildew with the new retractable Vineyard Dome. Based on the same technology used in the new Toronto stadium, the Dome provides the grower with a worry-free growing season.

Iced Tea Wine. Every time I go to a restaurant for lunch, I see table after table of iced tea, and precious few with wine. So, we make a wine that looks like iced tea, tastes good with ice and a lemon wedge and sell it cheap. That should get people back on the bottle.

Finally, *The Jake Lorenzo Wine Columns,* the collected works of Jake Lorenzo, including columns rejected by the powers that be and interviews like nothing you've ever seen before. Look for details in the next issue of *Practical Winery and Vineyard.*

Fight to make your fantasies into realities, Jake does. Keep the realities fun and affordable. When someone tells you you've gone to far, laugh hysterically and take another step.

I leave you with one more fantasy that we can all turn into reality. As an industry let's advertise that anyone who votes and shows up in our tasting rooms on election day with their voting stub, gets a free glass of wine of their choice.

After all, given the candidates and their ladders, America needs a drink on election day.

A MODEST PROPOSAL

I'll tell you the truth. I read the paper almost every day, but I only read the sports section and sometimes the movie section.

I mention this because while reading the paper I had a revelation, one of those flashes of insight that clearly and concisely focuses all the disparate elements in your life into a simple truth.

Of course, such revelations are fleeting, and virtually impossible to pass on, as you are about to see.

Actually, I was minding the counter at Chuy's Burrito Palace. Chuy was attending a meeting of local restaurateurs and bar owners who were bemoaning the current tragic state of their business. They were putting the blame squarely at the feet of the neo-prohibitionists, the cops busting people for drunk driving, and video merchants.

I had finished the Sporting Green and was into the movie section, when I saw the listing of the top ten TV shows.

Revelation struck.

I don't watch any of the top ten TV shows. Not in America. Not even in San Francisco. And that's not all: I don't like white zin, I don't drink wine coolers, and none of the politicians I vote for ever get elected. I'm out of the mainstream of American life.

That got me to thinking about freedom. By freedom, I'm talking about freedom of choice. Freedom of choice is a most precious commodity. Accordingly, Jake Lorenzo treats it with great respect, and I am distressed when I see it squandered.

Freedom of choice has two enemies and one catch.

The first enemy is poverty. You don't have a choice if your baby is starving, or if you can't get necessary medical care, or if you have no place to sleep. The second enemy is ignorance. You can't choose what you don't know. People who have never seen a steak rarely order one, and people don't visit places they don't know about.

We are fortunate in America. For the most part, we have defeated the enemies of freedom. Most of us are not hungry, and most of us have the opportunity to acquire knowledge.

In America, we suffer from the catch. When you make a choice, you have to take responsibility for the consequences.

The catch scares the hell out of a lot of people. Making a choice and being responsible for the consequences is too terrifying. Instead, they look for other people to tell them what to do, what to eat, what to wear, and what to think. They squander their freedom.

The backside of this phenomenon is equally frightening. When there are hordes of people looking to be told what to do, others take it upon themselves to direct them. They quickly assume that they have a right to enforce their opinions on the rest of us.

Frankly, that pisses Jake Lorenzo off. As I've said, I take my freedom of choice pretty seriously, and I sure as hell am not going to give it up without a fight.

Now, I've already admitted to being out of the mainstream, but see if this makes sense.

Professionally, I'm a private eye, but in the rest of my life, I'm a social animal. I like to be with other people. I like to share food with other people, and I like to drink. I seriously enjoy a fine meal with a couple of bottles of wine. Often, I am slightly over the legal limit and shouldn't drive home, but I have no convenient alternatives. We have few cabs, none late at night. We have no buses after dark. My house is too far to walk, and usually the people with me have also been imbibing.

Some people opt for staying home and renting a video, instead of going out on the town. That's fine, but it's tough on my friends in the restaurant and bar business.

I'm not advocating that we allow the drunks to continue their slaughter on the country's highways, but I resent having my freedom of choice infringed upon. I resent having my lifestyle attacked. The anti-drunk driving people have missed the point. We need to get drunk drivers out of their cars and off the streets. It's not a crime to drink. It's not a crime to get drunk. Getting behind the wheel of a car while intoxicated shows poor judgment (and may lead to disastrous results), but it is not a criminal act.

Right now, we must be wary. The police may not be able to catch criminals, but they can catch you. They are on the streets and highways of our state, and they can't wait to nail you. This leads to lots of embarrassment, inconvenience and expense. It jams our overflowing court system, and it crowds our overcrowded jails. But, as statistics prove, the one thing it does *not* do is get the drunk driver off the streets.

I have a better idea. Stop treating people who enjoy drinking like criminals. Provide them with an agreeable and convenient alternative to driving home. Develop a program that will educate and enlighten, instead of threaten and punish.

Here's how: We must provide alternatives to driving home while intoxicated. Since I am a great believer in experiential education, I would prefer that guilty drunk drivers be forced to do community service. They would report to police stations with their own vehicles.

As people in restaurants, bars and at parties found themselves too inebriated to drive, they would call their local police station. One of the community service drivers (CSD) would be dispatched to take the people where they had to go.

Police stopping inebriated drivers would need only write a ticket. If no one in the car is capable of driving, the officer can summon a CSD. CSDs would work shifts well into the morning, and could take people back to their cars and send them off to work.

The beauty of this plan is that it not only keeps the drunks off the road, but it allows the CSDs to confront drunken, obnoxious, puking behavior, and gives them the opportunity to learn from the experience. Since there would be no need to drive when intoxicated, those who continued to do so could more easily be targeted as problem drinkers and guided to the proper agencies with their problems.

Objections to the plan, would no doubt be many, but most are nonsense. Insurance problems and administrative costs could be covered by small fines from the CSDs, and from contributions from the liquor and service industries. The program would allow for tremendous savings in court costs, jailing expense, lost man hours and paper work. It would free cops to chase real criminals *and* it would keep drunk drivers off the road.

Unfortunately, there is one valid objection. Cab drivers are not into experiential education as much as I. Therefore, in those areas where there is adequate cab service, fines would be higher, CSDs would not operate, and cabs would be summoned to drive people from one place to another. The drivers would be paid from the collected fines.

Jake Lorenzo is for freedom of choice. I choose to be humane and effective. Chuy says he'll drive me home, so, if you don't mind, I think I'll have one more shot of Hornitos. Enjoy, and don't drive drunk.

WELCOME COMPANION

You know, the current hard economic times affect everyone, not just people in the wine business. If you think it is tough selling wine out there, imagine what it is like trying to earn a living as a private eye these days.

Sure, the murder rate is up, but doesn't it always seem to be some drug dealer in a drive-by shooting, or some lunatic who snaps and wipes out the local McDonald's, or some serial killer making human meat pies.

Whatever happened to the simple planned murder to get at the insurance or to get rid of an unwanted husband or wife? When was the last time you heard of one of those convoluted blackmail schemes gone awry only to be thwarted by the elegant, wisecracking detective? Those were the kinds of problems that could be handled by a trained private eye, such as myself.

I'm telling you, there's nothing simple about trying to get someone to ante up $250 per diem plus expenses in this recessionary economy. Even the detective's staple, adulterous detecting, has taken a nose dive in this AIDS conscious culture.

Don't get me wrong. I'm not complaining. After all, Jake Lorenzo is an experienced, well known throw back to all the movie private dicks you've ever seen. I'm doing alright, but now that I've celebrated my 45th birthday, I have been giving my future some thought.

Since Jakelyn only has one more year at college, which will greatly relieve my current financial burden, and since Jakelyn's mother and I are still getting along pretty good after all these years, I have been studying potential career changes for my future years.

Carl Sandburg wrote "Time is the coin of your life, be careful lest others spend it for you." I've always tried to spend my precious moments in the most pleasurable way. As a result, I've been pretty satisfied with most of my life, but I can't tell you the times I've met people with lots more money than I, who just seem plain miserable. They've got sail boats, private planes, condos in the mountains, luxurious shacks on the Thai coast, but they never seem to have the time to enjoy them.

Enter Jake Lorenzo, welcome companion.

Jake Lorenzo is a charming curmudgeon. He's well read, loves fine food, and knows good wines. He's traveled around the world, speaks a smattering of several foreign languages, loves music and dancing till all hours. Jake is now available to help you enjoy all that expensive crap you've been working so hard to acquire.

Want to take that sailboat out, feel the wind blowing across your face, suck down a few cold brewskies as your lips chap? Call Jake, he'll lift the mainsail.

Want to get out in the sloughs, drop a line in the water, watch the birds fly overhead while we try for that giant sturgeon? Call Jake, he loves drinking on boats.

Want to get up to the cabin, hit the slopes and then come home for a steak and some red wine in front of a roaring fire? Jake's ready to learn how to ski, knows how to barbecue and will even shovel your walkway just for the exercise.

Get the idea? A welcome companion is a great concept. Jake Lorenzo is a guy just friendly enough and interesting enough and funny enough to take along on almost any trip to any destination on any mode of transportation.

Just one disclaimer, I'm not much of a camper. Jake Lorenzo's idea of camping is passing out at a rustic bar, indoors, in lumber country. It's not that I'm against nature. I love nature. I revel in the majesty of the redwoods. I enjoy the murmur of a babbling brook. I am thrilled by sunsets near any body of water, but hiking through forests, and eating freeze-dried food is not my cup of tea.

In fact, on those rare occasions when I have a cup of tea, I like it to taste like tea, not flowers, or perfume. In much the same way, when I have a glass of wine, I like it to taste like wine, not like the toasted insides of some majestic oak tree grown in some verdant forest in the center of France.

I don't consider myself a connoisseur, but I do know the difference between a dish subtly accented by different spices and seasonings and that same dish hopelessly floundering in piles of garlic. I know the difference between a salsa concocted of different chilies so that complex, exotic flavors burn through the fire, and a bowl of chopped up jalapenos, onions and tomatoes that is all heat and no flavor.

I know that, in general, novices are most appreciative of a single prominent flavor. However, as their palates learn about food and wine, they are more able to pick out and appreciate the subtleties. They begin to understand balance. They recognize the essence of the main ingredient, but they appreciate the seasonings attending it.

In wine, grapes are the main ingredient. Fermentation techniques, barrel usage, and blending are simply the seasonings. That is why I cannot for the life of me understand why so many supposed experts still confuse the seasoning with the main ingredient. I can't understand why people will spend $25-$60 for oak, seasoned with grape juice, when they can buy some truly lovely wine, accented with oak, for half the price.

In the February 1992 issue of *Connoisseurs' Guide* there is an extensive review of Sauvignon Blanc. Looking at the several offerings receiving three puffs, you can read the following: "Abundant oak takes an early lead in the intensely toasty aromas... Although this ample wine's billowy oak seems at first to steal the show...Creamy oak serves as a most attractive counterpoint...Lots of toasty oak and dried brush elements..." I am not singling out the *Connoisseurs' Guide*. All of the review publications have this sweet tooth for oak. So, it seems, do most of the current judges awarding medals.

It may be that current taste has passed me by, but something has to be wrong when wineries spend more money for oak than they do for the source material of grapes. Depending on the variety, grape costs average $900 to $1400 per ton. Figuring 160 gallons to the ton, and $550 to $600 per French oak barrel, the price for new oak is $1600 to $1800 per ton.

This makes no sense. It is like spending $20 per pound for fine aged steaks flown in from Chicago, and then spending $40 for the charcoal to barbecue them.

Now, Jake Lorenzo is not saying that there's anything wrong with intense wines loaded with toasty oak flavors. I am saying that those of us with experience and expertise should differentiate between a wine loaded up with oak and those wines delicately accented and balanced with a melange of aromas and flavors. We should, in short, appreciate the difference between a dish overloaded with garlic and the same dish balanced with garlic, basil, parsley, salt and pepper.

Oak flavored wine is becoming the fast food equivalent in the premium wine market. Load that wine up with new oak and the critics will rhapsodize over it. Overpower the fruit with lovely toasty aromas and the public will wait in line to hand you their money.

But don't mistake that for the art of making fine wine. After all, great chefs are not hanging out at McDonald's trying to steal recipes.

WORMS

More than 20 years ago, I had a friend who taught in East Los Angeles. One day he was giving a science lesson. On his desk stood two empty glasses. One, he filled with water. The other, he filled with wine.

From a small wooden box he pulled two wiggling worms. He dropped the first worm into the glass of water where it wiggled around like a kid in a pool on a hot day. The second worm was dropped into the glass of wine where it immediately turned rigid and died.

My friend posed the question to his class. "Class," he said, "What have we learned from this experiment?"

Deep in the back row a kid's hand shot up and he said, "It goes to prove that if you drink wine, you ain't gonna get no worms."

   *   *   *

Most of the time Jake Lorenzo is upbeat. I'm a positive, optimistic person with a bizarre sense of humor. I find some of the oddest things funny. On the other hand, I am often devastated by things that never seem to bother the people around me.

In this column, Jake Lorenzo is going to vent his spleen.

Way back when Jake Lorenzo was in college, my hero was Abbie Hoffman. We started up a Guerrilla Theater group. Our theater ranged from the absurd, like giving out free oranges stolen from the orange groves that the school wanted to tear down, thereby thwarting the evil administrators' plot to give the students scurvy; to the

72

more dramatic showing of films of burning napalmed Vietnamese children on the cafeteria walls during lunch time, which resulted in having the football team beat the crap out of us.

That's what Guerrilla Theater was about: disrupting day to day reality in funny or shocking ways to force people to consider things that hadn't entered their minds.

So I've got to ask, "Who the hell is Jay Conrad Levinson, and what does he have against humor?" The wine business has become the snobbiest, most humorless, most depressed industry in America. Some guy who dares to invent Guerrilla Marketing (a surreal-dadaistic term if ever I heard one) advises the industry to avoid humor. *PMV* Nov/Dec 1991) Dunk this guy in a glass of wine and see if he wiggles.

* * *

As I remember it, when the real California wine boom began in the '70s, it derived much of its energy from the joining together of very incongruous groups of people.

It was hippies and other disenfranchised people searching for a more rural and natural life for their families and children who moved into the sleepy towns and hamlets of northern California and became cellar rats for the burgeoning wine industry.

It was intelligent, successful, caring professionals disgusted by the greed and callousness of business who opted to start their own small wineries and leave the rat race behind.

It was local farmers looking, as all farmers do, for a viable crop and a secure market who decided to protect themselves by starting their own wineries.

73

It was the poor and hungry laborers from Mexico, desperate for money to feed their families who were willing to do the backbreaking work in the fields.

So, hippies (who thought all farmers were redneck bigots); farmers (who thought long hairs were sex crazed communists); professionals (who were simultaneously terrorized and invigorated by the risk they were taking); and Mexican laborers (intent on feeding their families) combined to produce this magical melange that energized the wine business.

Hippies were thrilled to earn a living so connected to the seasons and nature. Farmers were thrilled with the easy, informal, funloving, hardworking cellar rats. They were re-energized by this younger generation that respected them for protecting the earth and producing this bounty from Mother Nature. Mexican laborers earned enough money to feed their families, bring them to California and offer them a better life in the future. Professionals heaved a sigh of relief to see that risk taking had been worth it, that success was just around the corner and could be had without sacrificing ideals in the name of profit.

Well, ladies and gentlemen of the wine industry, you had better lift your noses from those depressing computerized depletion sheets. Look around. We must be ever vigilant or we will find that we have become the enemy.

*   *   *

It's been almost a year since I told you about my friend Kieran Toovey. His father Tracy was a great winemaker and a good friend. Kieran wasn't even a year old when his father was murdered.

I asked every winery to send a bottle or two of their 1988 releases to set up a wine library for Kieran. During the year I've contacted winery associations, tasting groups, and private parties to donate to Kieran's Cellar. You know how many of the more than 700 wineries in California took the time and went through the expense of sending a bottle or two of wine to this wonderful child? FIFTEEN!

That is a pathetic and callous showing from an industry purported to have a heart.

Do yourself a favor. Get up and send the damn bottle right this minute. Send it to:

Kieran's Cellar
c/o Jake Lorenzo
17090 Park Ave.
Sonoma, CA 95476

Then call a couple of your cohorts in the wine business and badger them until they send a bottle.

*   *   *

Sometimes we find ourselves sitting at a table filled with $30 bottles of wine. In the midst of the laughter and good company a dark thought passes through our brain.

We're not enjoying this fine wine nearly as much as we used to. The flavors turn our mouths chalky and we can't think beyond the next interest payment, or the next wine review. We can't enjoy the sprawling vista of vineyards without worrying about phylloxera. Our kids have grown up too fast and we wish we had spent more time watching them.

Take a hint from your friend, Jake Lorenzo. The American bible, 60 Minutes, tells us that drinking wine with your meals is good for you. We all realize that our veins are like freeways by now, and those platelets don't stand a chance in hell of sticking to the walls.

We've got plenty of time.

We can think about what's truly important to us, to our families, and for our planet. If the wine industry will no longer allow us to pursue what we truly believe, then we have two choices: we can change it back to what we want, or we can leave it and look for a new challenge.

Either choice is viable.

Whichever way you go, don't forget that magical melange of energy that forced itself into the bottle. Wine will always be a part of our lives.

And we can rest assured knowing we ain't gonna get no worms.

PART III

Wine
Industry
At Large

IN THE BEGINNING

In the beginning there was Al Brett at Buena Vista, and Al Brett trained four sons: Don and Steve and Val and Charlie. One day, the bosses said unto Al, "Al, even though it is harvest, even though you and your sons are working more hours than are in a day, even though the grapes are coming in and coming in, you are not to crush until we arrive with the Muckety Mucks from the Land of Sales."

So Al waited, and Al's sons waited with him. And they waited. And they still waited. Finally, the Muckety Mucks from the Land of Sales arrived with the Bosses. Al directed his sons to hoist the gondola of grapes. Slowly, ever so slowly it rose, until just at the fulcrum, it sat, not spilling the grapes, but ever so ready to spill them.

Al spoke to his sons. "Sons, follow me," and he took them to town and fed them ice cream while the muckety mucks from the Land of Sales and the bosses watched the gondola not dump its cargo of grapes. Thus did Al train his sons.

In the time of Al, there was the house of Sebastiani, which sat behind tall invisible walls, so no one knew what took place there. And high on the mountain in the center of town was a beautiful paradise known as Hanzell and run by Brad Webb, who begat Bob Sessions.

To the East in the land of Vineburg were the brothers-in-law Bundschu, who re-started Gundlach Bundschu. Then they had bitter arguments. So John went to Bandiera, and Barney went to Chateau St. Jean, and the land was left to Jim Bundschu and Lance Cutler.

Also in the East was the house of ZD, where Gino Zepponi and Norm DeLeuze had their humble beginnings. They journeyed to the land of Napa, where Norm moved to the Silverado Trail, and Gino begat the first house of sparkling wine in California. Alas, Gino was lost on the roads in the Land of Sales.

In the meantime, Buena Vista's Al Brett was lost, and his sons were scattered through the Valley. In the center, Don planted the vines that became Hacienda, which begat Crawford Cooley and Steve MacRostie. The house of Sebastiani continued to live behind the invisible walls, so no one knew what went on there, but rumblings were heard. And the bosses at Buena Vista sold to men from the Land of Sales, who in turn sold to people from the German drug company.

To the West came Prince Arrowood, who had studied at the feet of Rodney the Strong. The Prince began Chateau St. Jean and took Al Brett's son, Charlie, to run his kingdom. And Charlie ran it so well that he left to run his own kingdom at Haywood. He turned Chateau St. Jean over to his brother Don, who had started the vineyards at Hacienda.

Also in the West came the brothers Lee, who hired Al's other sons, Steve and Val, to run their kingdom. And they thrived especially with the addition of Mark and Jeff who have stayed and stayed and stayed.

And between the lands of Chateau St. Jean and Kenwood began the kingdom of St. Francis, who had none of Al's sons to help him and so Joe Martin foundered until the coming of Tom Mackey.

Further up the road, lay the Grand Cru, ruled by Bob Magnani and Al Ferrara, who wisely hired Tracy Toovey to run their kingdom. Tracy came from Buena Vista (after Al, but before the German drug company). And Grand Cru prospered, until it was sold to the Baron of Bread, Walter Dreyer, who slowly lost market share.

Then the brave Tracy was murdered and Grand Cru was gobbled up by the Bronco.

Meanwhile, numerous small kingdoms were started, and their names were Laurel Glen and Matanzas Creek and Ravenswood and Richardson, and without anybody noticing, the land changed. The apples left the land. And the pears. And the prunes. And soon there was nothing but grapes. Grapes and tourists.

In the center of town, the invisible walls of Sebastiani tumbled down, the result of a brotherly battle on the order of Cain and Abel. One brother was left with the kingdom, while the other moved to the far land of Schellville to begin Viansa. Once Schellville was graced by the kingdom of Viansa, it attracted the houses of Roche and Cline and MacRostie. That left Crawford and Hacienda, who were gobbled up by the Bronco.

Haywood, and Herr Stemmler from the Land of Alexander, were gobbled up by the German drug company. Al Brett's son Charlie was cast adrift to wash up on the shore of the land of Benziger.

Meanwhile, Chateau St. Jean was left with Al's son Don, but was sold to the Japanese liquor house of Suntory. So Prince Arrowood left to begin his own kingdom.

Nearby, Kenwood lost Al's son Steve, who went to the land of Hanna, and eventually left the business of wine. Al's remaining son Val, left Kenwood and drifted until he too arrived on the shores of the land of Benziger, where he now runs the house of Vallejo.

St. Francis has been sold, but retains the services of the loyal Tom. Landmark has moved in, after being tossed out of their native land by encroaching housing tracts. Matanzas Creek bought its way out of the valley and into the County. Laurel Glen grew under the hand of the trusty Ray Kaufman, friend to Lance Cutler.

Wellington blossoms, started by a father and son who escaped from the land of Sebastiani when the wall tumbled. Kunde prospers using the grapes once sold to Sebastiani. B.R. Cohn waves his banner on the highway.

Ravenswood has moved into the house of Haywood, whose name was lost to the German drug company, even though Ravenswood's good Little John Kemble went to seek his fortune in the land of New Zealand. Hanzell clings to its paradise due only to the tenacious dedication of Brave Bob Sessions. The House of Bundschu is under siege by the dark knights of the Police. The Caves of Carmenet have been rented to public stock options.

And there is more, much more, but I have neither the time, nor the stomach to continue.

All this has come to pass in just 20 short years. Already, Al is forgotten except by his sons. Gino and Tracey bring scarcely a mention. More and more, the bosses and the ravenous Bronco and the men from the Land of Sales control the land.

Jake Lorenzo says you must record the history. You must pass on the truth. We cannot leave the story to Japanese liquor companies, German drug companies, or pretenders to the throne. Our time will come again. One day, a child will hoist a gondola. It will sit with the grapes ready to fall, but not falling, with the crush ready to begin, but not beginning. And we will take a moment to have ice cream with our past.

THE DEAL

Talk to a winemaker. He'll set down his wine glass and tell you, "It's all in the grapes. Good grapes make good wine. God bless the grape grower."

Talk to a grape grower. He'll take a piece of straw out of his mouth and say, "Shucks, I just grow the little fellas. That there winemaker, he's the one turns 'em into wine. God bless the winemaker."

It makes for nice PR, but it's hardly reality. The true relationship between grape grower and winemaker is far from the idyllic one they would have us believe. In fact, grape growers and winemakers are constantly at war. The heart of the conflict revolves around economics and battles rage over the complex system of payment. Only the ability to negotiate an equitable peace makes for fine wines.

The whole thing starts peacefully enough. The grower and the winemaker enter into a deal. The grower will grow the best wine grapes in the county, and the winemaker will take those grapes and make the finest wine to ever grace the inside of a bottle.

Since the grower is going to grow the best grapes in the county, the winemaker generously offers him $1400 per ton, instead of $1250. The grower, not to be outdone by this generosity, tells the winemaker that he will do whatever the winemaker deems necessary to assure that his grapes live up to their rightful destiny.

That's fine with the winemaker, who just happens to have a few suggestions. You see, the winemaker knows that the best wines come from low yielding grapes. With healthy vines, lower yields mean more intensity in the grapes, higher sugars, better acids, and more varietal character. He explains all this to the grower, and pours more wine to prove his point.

The grower looks at the winemaker like he's got a case of sunstroke. "You want me to grow *less* grapes?"

You see the grower is sitting on a 100 acre vineyard, which cost $20,000 per acre to develop, *not* counting the price of the raw land, with maintenance costs of $1000 per acre per year.

He pushes aside his glass of wine, pours himself a bourbon and water, and explains that a $2,000,000 investment with fixed costs of $100,000 per annum requires that he produce 5 tons per acre just to break even.

The winemaker groans, "Five tons per acre. I'll be lucky to make jug wine. I'm talking gold medals here. I'm talking blue ribbons. I'm talking your vineyard name on the label."

"Vineyard designation is nice, but the only way I can do it is with a bonus. I could cut the yield, but you'd have to pay a bonus for each tenth above 22° Brix up to a total 20% bonus."

"All right, you cutthroat, but if you overcrop, or pull any of that late irrigation, it's going to cost you 1% penalty for each tenth below 22° Brix up to a 20% penalty, with additional penalties for MOG, bunchrot, and botrytis."

It goes on and on throughout the growing season. They argue about how many canes are left on each vine, how many buds are left on each cane, how many times and when to irrigate. They fight about the sugars and the acids, when to pick and how to pick, and finally, they argue about the test sample.

The winemaker will tell you that if it wasn't for his genius, the grapes wouldn't have made decent vinegar, let alone fine wine. The grape grower will tell you that his grapes were so good, a chimpanzee could have won medals.

Maybe it's not a war. Perhaps, we should look upon their relationship as a system of checks and balances. When the checks don't bounce, and the balances work out just right, then we all enjoy the fruits of their labor.

HEAD OF SECURITY

I shivered in the fierce cold of Candlestick Park.
My nearly empty bottle of Hornitos wasn't helping, and I
had lost the feeling in my toes before half-time. The
crowd was unusually drunk, which was typical for a
Sunday night game.

The more the Atlanta Falcons thrashed the 49ers,
the more belligerent became the crowd. The call came
over my walkie talkie, "Head of Security to Section 8.
Code Blue." I drained the half pint and hurried over.

He was huge, at least 6'8" and about 260 lbs. His
shirt was off and sweat glistened from his rippling
muscles, in spite of the bone numbing cold. He was
whipping a large pipe wrench through the air, and three
of my security guards were on the ground bleeding. I
pulled my gun and dropped the guy with a leg shot.

I figured my quick thinking had saved a nasty
situation from getting worse, but it didn't play out that
way. As my boss put it, "We can't have our Head of
Security shooting the fans." Quick thinking had cost me
my job.

I had just sized up the situation, and tried to do my
job. It was nothing personal.

Winemaking, on the other hand, is extremely
personal. Wines reflect the personality and philosophy of
the winemaker, just as much as they reflect the grapes
from which they are produced. In addition, consumers
select wines based on carefully calculated prejudices.

As a consumer, I much prefer wines made by "real"
winemakers. A real winemaker, to my way of thinking, is
a person with a worn pair of rubber boots. His hands are

stained black from grape acid during *CRUSH*. He has great respect and appreciation for cellar rats, and he never asks me to work on a divorce case.

A good example is Arnold Tudal of Tudal Winery. Arnold is a transplanted farmer now growing grapes and making wine just north of St. Helena. He is a meticulous, enthusiastic and good natured man. His vineyard is manicured to the point of elegance, and so is his cabernet sauvignon.

Nobody ever heard of Charlie Tolbert when he worked in the cellar at Chateau St. Jean. From there he went on to become winemaker at Haywood Winery. Currently, he is one of the winemakers for Benziger Winery. For almost 20 years Charlie Tolbert has quietly gone about producing some of Sonoma Valley's finest wines.

Last year, I spent an entire afternoon talking to and tasting with John Parducci. There's a real dynamo. He's opinionated, dedicated, and still excited by winemaking. He dragged me through the whole winery, tasting samples, talking about vintages, oak, technique. When you finish with John Parducci, you've got to stop just to catch your breath, but year after year he keeps producing fine modestly-priced wines.

The winemaker's art is sensitivity, for a winemaker must be sensitive to the nuance of the grape, to the balance of the fruit, to the flavor of the oak. Individual personalities influence this sensitivity and are reflected in the finished wines. John Parducci's wines are different from Arnold Tudal's or Charlie Tolbert's as much because of the people who made them as the grapes from which they were made.

Differences are what makes the wine business so exciting. But differences may also be the undoing of some winemakers at this year's ASE convention in Reno. Despite what you might hear, Reno is not at all like a cellar. Reno is gambling, drinking, sex and glitter: Jake Lorenzo territory.

The first thing to realize when you get to Reno is that you are not famous winemakers. In Reno, you are conventioneers. Winemakers, Elks Club, Daughters of the American Revolution-- it makes no difference in Reno. A conventioneer is a conventioneer.

A conventioneer is also a prospective gambler. Prospective gamblers are prospective losers, and losers pay the freight. Remember, the voluptuous waitress wearing the costume no larger than your label is not plying you with free drinks because she's a fan of a famous winemaker.

Remember, casinos may give credit easier than Production Credit Banks, but they have a much different late payment policy. No matter how much you plead and beg, casinos are not likely to take all that cabernet piled up in your warehouse in lieu of your gambling debts. So have fun, and if you see Jake Lorenzo, buy him a drink.

LIVING THINGS

When you wake up and find yourself sleeping on the ground as often as I do, you tend to develop a love and respect for the land. Land, as any farmer will tell you, can be rich and bountiful, but farming that land can be frustrating, fruitless and financially disastrous.

The farmer's day is long, hot and dusty. Things constantly break down and need repair. Crops are continually threatened by bizarre weather conditions, a myriad of insects and diseases, and the dreaded tractor blight. Even when the farmer has done his job and the crop is ready, a capricious market can spoil a whole year's harvest.

Obviously, farmers are a special breed of people. Since the wine industry is so dependent upon the success of the grape farmers, I felt this column was in order. Remember, however, that I am a private investigator trained to see below the surface. When I speak of farmers, I am not necessarily talking about the guy whose name is on the label. I'm talking about the guy driving the tractor, the guy walking the rows, the guy with sulfur up his nose.

Look at today's wineries and you will find that the best of them, those whose wines actually improve year after year, have someone special managing their vineyards. These are the unsung heroes of the wine industry. Their diligence and talent determines the quality of the raw material given to the winemaker. And it is the quality of the fruit, after all, that most affects the quality of the finished wine.

Ferrari Carano is a new winery that burst upon the scene, a full blown success. Don Carano is a man of vision, and George Bursick is a capable winemaker, but the man bringing in the fruit since the inception of the winery is none other than Barney Fernandez.

For years, Barney was the vineyard manager for Chateau St. Jean. People raved about Robert Young's vineyard, and Belle Terre and McRae Ranch. While the owners of those vineyards are fine farmers in their own right, Barney was the go-between, the conduit from farmer to winemaker, from the field to the crusher.

Barney is boisterous, fun-loving and loud. He knows a hell of a lot about grapes and their care, and may be California's leading expert on botrytis in the vineyard. Barney shuns the publicity and hoopla of the wine business, but it is no coincidence that Ferrari Carano hit the market running, with full-bodied complex wines. Barney has been far too valuable a factor in that success to escape my detective's eye.

Jesus "Chuy" Ordaz cooks the best birria in Sonoma Valley. He also manages the vineyards for Kenwood Vineyards. John Sheela, president of Kenwood Vineyards, says, "Chuy is a great manager of manpower. His ability to organize a crew, get the grapes picked at the right time and to the winery as quickly as possible, has had a lot to do with our ability to improve the quality of our wines."

Chuy's crew is legendary in Sonoma Valley. The entire crew has been know to sing songs while sprinting down the rows with full lugs of grapes on their heads. Chuy is a leader of men, and a master of the vine.

Chuy manages, single-handedly, a crew of over 60 men and women, and is largely responsible for the quality of fruit delivered to Kenwood Vineyards. He has held this vital position for more than 15 years, but when was the last time you heard or read about Chuy Ordaz?

Rhinefarm Vineyards and Gundlach Bundschu Winery have been around for 135 years. Since the winery's rebirth in 1973, Marcelo Hernandez has managed the 350 acres of grapes. According to owner Jim Bundschu, "Marcelo is entrusted with the grapes and their health. He is responsible for doing everything necessary to provide the winery with the finest grapes possible. Fortunately, for Gundlach Bundschu, he is very good at doing just that."

Marcelo is a hardworking and creative farmer who insists on doing things right the first time. He spent three years working in the winery during *CRUSH* to better understand the problems and frustrations of winemaking. His shift from cane to cordon pruning of Rhinefarm's merlot coincided with, and obviously contributed to, Gundlach Bundschu's tremendous success with that varietal.

Farming, winemaking and research go hand in hand. Researchers analyze grapes and wines down to microscopic components. They study nitrogen, potassium and chemical build up in the soil and vine. They examine pH, TA and phenolics in wine. They have used microscopes, telescopes, radar, HPLC and voodoo, but the secret to great wine remains a mystery.

I am not an expert in any scientific sense. I am not berating the valuable and important technical research being done, but my detective's nose tells me that the real secret lies elsewhere.

Grapes and wines are living things. Living things relate to and interact with the world around them. In large part, vines and wines become what they do because of the people who care for them.

Barney, Chuy, and Marcelo maintain a special relationship with the vines in their care and they provide a link between the field and the winery. Each puts his indelible mark on the finished wine.

Jake Lorenzo would like to suggest that the secret to great wines lies in the people who make them.

LAWS OF GREAT
WINEMAKING

The monotonous, clanking, never ending line of bottles has finally ended. The winery takes on its preparatory gleam. Excitement fills the air. The hour of the winemaker is at hand.

All the knowledge, technical know how, experience and flaky ideas must blend together and translate themselves into picking dates, skin contact time and fermentation temperatures. Bees abound, CO_2 fills the air, and the strain of long hours and split-second decisions create the heady intoxication of *CRUSH*.

CRUSH is the foundation, the cornerstone of all the wines to come. The winemaker's talent, drive and creativity exert their greatest influence. In the beginning, the goal is to make great wines. By the end, mere survival is often enough. *CRUSH* is Jake Lorenzo's idea of a good time, and in honor of good times, this column is directed to winemakers.

I take for granted that you are all primed and ready for the *CRUSH*, and that you are technically current with procedure, that your equipment is ready, your crew is ready and that you are fired up to make some great wines.

What I am about to pass on is based upon my belief that vines and grapes are living beings with a life and a destiny of their own, Vines, grapes and wines interact with and are influenced by the people who tend them.

For a grape, the winemaking process is like the metamorphosis of a caterpillar to butterfly. It is that exquisite moment that the winemaker must preserve, care for, and transfer to the bottle.

Keeping that in mind, I present Jake Lorenzo's Laws of Great Winemaking.

LAW #1: THE ONLY GOOD GRAPE IS A HAPPY GRAPE.

Grapes appreciate being rushed to the winery and crushed safely into clean tanks to begin the fermentation process. They thrive on the care and concern you show them.

This law would appear to be self-evident, but it is often overlooked by harried wine makers. The above mentioned metamorphosis from vine to wine is not necessarily a pleasant experience for a grape.

It involves, after all, that grapes be torn from the vines that nurtured them, thrown into gondolas, dumped, crushed, pressed, dusted with chemicals, chilled and then fermented. This sort of treatment could seriously upset a grape.

The key here is for the winemaker to make things as comfortable as possible for the grapes as they are subjected to the rigors of fermentation. Grapes are sensitive and observant. They prefer being picked in the cool of the morning and being placed in clean gondolas.

LAW #2: PUT YOUR HOUSE IN ORDER BEFORE YOU INVITE A GRAPE.

Grapes interact with and are influenced by the people around them. Therefore, it is critical that the winemaker, his crew and anyone else involved with the winemaking process be enthusiastic, content and interested.

In light of the long hours, high temperatures and extreme physical exertion imposed upon winery staff during *CRUSH*, it behooves the winemaker to provide for his people all that he can.

94

Hot meals, cold drinks, music, good humor and common sense go a long way toward bolstering spirits and maintaining commitment. Remember, everyone likes a party, even grapes.

LAW #3: EVERY CRUSH NEEDS A BEGINNING, A MIDDLE AND AN END.

CRUSH, as an event, is loaded with variables. The weather, the hours, the break downs are all variable. In such a situation, organization is a virtue.

Just as we like a good strong frost to snap the vines out of their dormancy, so does a great party get the juices flowing for *CRUSH*. Just as judicious irrigation will perk up droopy vines, so will a mid-*CRUSH* bash rejuvenate tired bodies. Just as harvest signals the end of a cycle for the vine, so does a pig roast or a tequila night signal the end of another vintage.

To sum up Law #3, anyone can get through *CRUSH* if you sleep at night. The challenge is to get through the *CRUSH* while doing the maximum of partying. The grapes will respect you for it.

LAW #4: IT TAKES A LOT OF GOOD BEER TO MAKE GREAT WINE.

If this law needs explaining, then you should get out of the wine business.

Finally, I would like to sincerely wish all of you a happy and successful *CRUSH*. Remember, should you require first class security or private investigation at any of your parties, you may reach me care of this magazine.

MEDALS

I've never been fond of medals. Somehow, they don't seem right without a uniform, and people who wear uniforms, especially those festooned with medals, are extremely rare in the wine country.

Judges wear robes. I guess robes are uniforms, but they would look ridiculous with medals dangling from them.

Judges are authority figures. That's why they can wear robes in the daytime without having people tease the hell out of them. In the wine business, judges don't wear robes, but they are still viewed as figures of authority.

Lacking uniforms, they have the good sense not to wear medals. Unfortunately, instead of wearing them, they spend a great deal of time giving them away.

According to John Parducci of Parducci Winery, "There are so many wineries and so many judgings that they're having a hell of a time finding enough qualified judges."

I'm not sure what the qualifications are to be a judge at a winetasting, but since I've been invited to several, I view all such proceedings with great suspicion.

Personally, I think the whole idea of judgings is ludicrous. Wine was meant to be drunk, usually with food, but nobody drinks at a judging. Go to an official judging and you are likely confronted by a table full of cabernets from five different vintages and 92 different wineries.

Faced with this plethora of wines, most judges look, smell, and then spit out one wine after another. When I participate in judgings, I don't spit. Put 92 cabernets in front of Jake Lorenzo and I'm going to taste each and every one of them.

When a tasting is over, all the other judges sit in front of the 92 full glasses and their bucket of wine and saliva with red stains on their chins where the wine dribbled.

I sit in front of a bunch of empty glasses, my spit bucket dry, my chin clear of all but the morning stubble. Never mind that my eyes are glazed and my cheeks are red.

Other judges complain about the buildup of tannins on their palates while they tally their points and make their awards. For me, it's simple; the empty glasses are the winners, the ones I didn't finish are the losers.

Of course, other judges criticize me for a general lack of professionalism, but who would you rather believe... a guy with wine dribbling down his chin or a very happy man with flushed cheeks? Besides, I never met a winemaker who said he went through all the trouble of making wine so that people could just spit it out.

This brings us to the question of validity. Can people, even professional winemakers, make accurate judgments when faced with 50 or even 150 wines?

Ken Brown of Byron Winery put it this way, "For the first 10-12 wines, I think judges can be fair and accurate, but as you taste more and more wines, you are less able to differentiate subtle differences in things like the levels of oak or alcohol."

Michael Martini of Louis Martini Winery feels that wines should not be compared one to the other. "Wines should be judged against a standard or ideal for that varietal, but in a judging situation, as you taste more wines, palate fatigue makes it more difficult to appreciate the softer, more drinkable wines."

In light of the difficulties and often questionable results inherent in these judgings, why do wineries participate? I got several interesting answers. Judgings promote wines and educate people about them. Competition builds quality. Winning satisfies the ego. But the bottom line, repeated by every winemaker was, "Medals sell wine."

Medals sell wine. Here we get to the heart of the matter. The wine business is, first and foremost, a business, and a very expensive, risky one at that.

The proliferation of new wineries, and the increased availability of imports has made retail shelves a jungle. The movement of wine sales away from small, service oriented shops to self-service chain stores only adds to the confusion.

Wineries, feeling the pinch of slowing sales, growing inventories and greatly increased competition are desperate for publicity. Therefore, they welcome the free publicity and attention generated by judgings, because they have all seen consumers clutching lists of medal winners while deciding which wines to purchase.

Now, Jake Lorenzo is a private eye. I'm not a judge. I don't own a uniform, and I've never won any medals, but I think the wine industry is making a big mistake.

Wine is a magical and unique commodity in the food and beverage industry. The very fact that wine judgings generate so much publicity proves that wine has a special attraction. After all, you don't read about milk tastings. No one seems to care about the pH of the apple they are eating.

The message that the industry sends to the consumer through these tastings is that there are winners and losers, that this wine is better than that one. Using this message to bolster sales is short-sighted, and in the long run, could prove disastrous.

Comparing wines to determine which is best is absurd, if not impossible, because it denies the very properties that make wine the magical commodity it is. Wines are not better *than* one another. They are *different* one *from* the other. The differences make wine special and help generate the magic.

If the wine industry is to build a solid foundation to support its growth, it would do well to emphasize differences between grape varieties, vintage conditions, appellations and vineyard designations.

If you must compare wines, then celebrate the differences between wines made in Napa Valley, Monterey and Mendocino. Rejoice in the differences. Don't denigrate one in favor of the other.

Just as every wine has a different taste and texture, each individual palate has certain likes and dislikes. Success for the wine industry lies not in attempting to define the best wine. It resides in helping each consumer to discover those wines he will enjoy most.

The buying public is starved for information and direction. Emphasize the glorious differences among wines. Describe those differences so the consumer can recognize them. Then let the consumer enjoy the thrill of discovery for himself.

Put the robes on the consumers. Give medals for the unique and varied magical properties of the product. Then rest assured that there are enough personal preferences to support all of our individual styles.

WINETASTING

The rain poured from the sky. The wind whipped the huge drops into heavy sheets and slammed them against the parked cars in front of Chuy's Burrito Palace.

I sat in my regular spot, the corner stool with the dark blood stain on the torn back cushion. The blood had been mine.

One of Chuy's ex-girlfriends, in the aftermath of a lovers quarrel, had tried to kill Chuy's huge bean pot. The pot laughed at the .22 slug and sent it spinning just past the tequila I was pouring into my morning coffee to nick me in the shoulder.

I didn't know I was hit until my Dizzy Gillespie for President T-shirt stuck to the back of the stool...no big deal. But Chuy embellished the story into some gigantic shootout that ended with me saving his undeserving life and since then no one has been allowed to sit in la silla de Jake, but Jake Lorenzo, himself.

On this cold and rainy morning, Chuy brought two steaming cups of black coffee. He poured a shot of Hornitos into each cup. We clanked the cups and drank.

"What you do today, Jake? Solve un pinche murder case?"

Chuy loved to talk like that. He said that it added to the Burrito Palace ambiance. He felt that the Palace's ambiance was the real reason for its great success. In fact, that's why he gave me free coffee and wouldn't let anyone else sit on the blood stained corner stool.

Once at my place, away from the Palace, Chuy reverted to his Cal Berkeley vocabulary and explained, "Maintaining the proper ambiance is the hardest part of any service business. Having Jake Lorenzo sitting there drinking tequila in his morning coffee lends a certain air of febricity and makes the Burrito Palace more exciting for the customers."

"So what gives, Jake? You gonna take mas fotografias of married girls cheating on their mens?" Chuy leered.

I stared out the window. The rain continued to pour. Streams of water raged alongside the curbs. I sipped the hot coffee, smiled and said, "Think I'll take the day off and go wine tasting."

Wine tasting, as everyone knows, has become California's top tourist attraction. Wherever tourists are attracted, businesses sprout eager to latch onto those tourist dollars. Restaurants open for hungry tourists. Motels and inns open for tired tourists. Cheese shops and delis open for picnicking tourists, and a wide assortment of stores and shops open for shopping tourists. All these businesses help to attract more and more tourists, but the real draw is still the winery tasting room (TPR in current BATF jargon.)

As more and more tourists filter into the area, the local people who are working in the sprouting tourist oriented businesses confront a dilemma. The same people they seek to attract to support their businesses are slowly and unknowingly destroying the very lifestyle that first caused them to be locals.

What was once a peaceful, rural valley is now a neon- flashing restaurant row. The wonderful neighborhood bakeries and delis now require 40 minute waits and the harried people behind the counters don't smile and can't shoot the shit any more. The lovely country roads are now jammed with traffic, and traffic lights are popping up like mushrooms after a warm November rain.

Nowhere is this dilemma more obvious than in the tasting rooms themselves. As little as two years ago, for those who sought them out, there were plenty of small, quiet wineries to visit, drink some wine, and have some friendly conversation.

Now, even those out-of-the-way wineries are inundated with bicycle clubs, tour buses, Porsche clubs and Rolls Royces. The friendly loquacious person behind the bar is so jaded by the tourist onslaught that a little conversation becomes a mine field with all sorts of hidden dangers.

I'm a detective, not a sociologist. So, I don't have the answer to this complex problem, but virtually every TPR has a bar, and when it comes to bars, detectives have a long history of experience and expertise. If you want to have a pleasant wine tasting experience, just follow these helpful hints:

1) Only go winetasting in the most miserable weather possible. This cuts down on crowds, affords you time to relax and talk with the TPR personnel, and allows you to approximate the chilling environment of cellar rats.

2) Don't be an idiot. Wines being poured are always displayed and/or listed, so don't ask what they're pouring. Price lists are always available, so don't ask what the prices are.

Before you ask how many grapes it takes to make a bottle of wine, or what the name of the owner's great grandmother was, or whether or not the wood for the barrels comes from the Disneyland forest, grab the newsletters and brochures and read what's in them.

3) Don't tell them what a great friend you are of the owner or winemaker or janitor.

4) Finally, while it's OK to skip some of the wines available, or to dump out some of each taste, it is incredibly poor taste to criticize, in any way, shape or form, the wine you are receiving free, while in the actual TPR giving it to you.

It has been my experience that most wineries have pretty good wines. What I enjoy most about a particular tasting room is the camaraderie of the bar, or, as Chuy would say, the ambiance.

You'll have the best wine tasting experience when you can open up and involve the person behind the bar. Try to realize how many times they've been asked the same question, and then don't ask those questions.

Since most of the people working in T.P.R.s love wine, it's easy to get information, but first you've got to build a personal relationship. That way it becomes interesting for every one involved.

WISDOM

I know detectives have a hard-nosed, tough-as-nails image, but if the truth be known, most of us are sentimentalists. The private eye business is often sleazy, corrupt and tawdry. It is occasionally violent. Hard edged cynicism is easy to come by.

I guess that is why I put so much faith and energy into friends. Good friends root you to the past and promise an interesting future. In thinking about my friends, I have found a common link, that all-important running thread in the fabric of my life.

Each of Jake Lorenzo's friends has a wonderful parent or grandparent to serve as a fount of wisdom. Lance Cutler's Baba had many insightful sayings, but the one Lance lives by is, "If you plant potatoes, you wouldn't get tomatoes."

Jim McCullough's grandmother used to say, "Jimmy, me boy, ye were cut out to be a gentleman, but the devil ran away wi' the pattern."

My own grandmother, Bertie, gave me advice that has saved me on more than one occasion. Bertie used to say, "Wound 'em first, then fight."

I guess what I'm talking about is history. A sense of it. A way of anchoring oneself in one's past so we can confidently steam ahead into the stormy waters of our future lives. Obviously, precious few of us live with these anchors. Too many people seem to bob on the waves, drifting with the currents, directionless. They lack that connection with their past, and drift aimlessly toward their future.

It's not the proper way to undertake a journey, yet it seems to describe a majority of the present wine industry.

Remember the early seventies? When grape growers and winemakers gathered, the conversation inevitably turned to grapes, clones and soils. Great discussions developed over which varieties to plant, where to plant them and how to grow them.

Later in the seventies, similar gatherings featured great arguments over winemaking technique. Skin contact, fermentation temperatures and fining procedures became common topics of discussion.

Whether the discussions centered on grape growing or winemaking, they were vociferous and invigorating. People argued and listened and mulled and made decisions. Conversation was based on confidence and curiosity. Participants took in information, evaluated it, and then acted upon it. It made for exciting times.

In the eighties, whenever people in the business got together, the topic for conversation was marketing and sales. Grapes and wine were out. Discounts, programming and PR were in. Nobody asked, "Who's your winemaker?" Instead, the question was, "Who's your distributor?"

Nowadays, things are even worse. All industry people do now is complain: rising costs, government interference, tin capsules, taxes, health issues.

It's not even that the topics for discussion have changed from grapes to marketing to complaining that bothers me. What bothers me is that the energy and confidence that characterized those early discussions has been replaced by a sense of helpless desperation, and desperate people rarely make bold, creative decisions.

The California wine industry of 15 years ago was directed by a rogue's gallery of strong-willed, stubborn, creative characters. Martin Ray, Joe Heitz, Joe Swann, Paul Draper, and Bob Mondavi knew exactly what they wanted to do and how they wanted to do it. They didn't care what others thought. They didn't listen to advice that said it couldn't be done. They simply did it the best they could.

These people, and others like them, gave the industry its direction, and their flamboyant personalities lent the industry a large portion of its romance. Winemaking, then, was a grand experiment, and the experiments weren't always successful. They were, however, unique and wildly creative.

Now, in the desperate days of slumping sales and marketing directors, even the industry giants are turning conservative. Supple, lively, well-balanced wines are fine, especially when done to perfection. Too often the sheep in the industry fail in their attempts, and we end up with over-fined, eviscerated wines that lack both charm and subtlety.

We need some young turks to say, "The tide be damned."

We need to hear more about those people making big, heavy, lush wines. People who take what they have learned about technique and apply it, to push winemaking farther out along the edge, instead of folding up into innocuous little wines that try to please everyone's palate.

Remember Jake's first law: Balance in all things.

The industry is losing its balance. The pendulum has swung too far. The future does not lie in producing a wine to please everyone. Success lies in producing a wide range of varied wines which can provide pleasure to a wide range of people with varied tastes.

Let personality reign. Let's not be sucked under by the unimaginative, frightened people. Let's go back to the vitality at the root of the industry.

HUMOR

Humor is an essential ingredient in the life of any good private investigator. Take my kind of work too seriously, and it can make you miserable. The greed and sleaze we often wallow in clogs the throat. It takes a healthy and heartfelt laugh to clear the breathing tubes.

Humor, at least a sense of it, is a good thing to pack when you take a trip. I just got back from two weeks on the road. Moving from town to town through airport after airport is exhausting. Road work makes me lethargic, too tired to think. When I'm too tired to think, I pursue mindless activities. I watch television.

Watch television for any length of time, and you'll see lots of commercials. Bartles and Jaymes crack me up. I like those guys. I think their commercials are fun and non-threatening. They have attracted a huge group of new consumers into the wine market. The Bartles and Jaymes producer is making lots of money.

Watching those two good old boys sitting on that there porch and talk about wine coolers fascinated Jake Lorenzo. My detective instinct was piqued. (That's the trouble with mindless activity; an active mind won't allow it.)

Questions popped into my head. Who the hell is drinking all these millions and millions of cases of wine coolers? Why don't I know one single person who has a bottle sitting in his refrigerator? What does the stuff taste like, anyway?

All detective work is simple, hard labor. Find the leads. Follow the leads. Make the obvious conclusions.

My questions led me to the nearest liquor store, where I bought a pile of wine coolers. I sat in my air conditioned hotel room with the ugly earth-toned prints on the wall, and I drank wine coolers. Wine coolers taste to me like health food soda pop that's gone bad.

The best that can be said for wine coolers is that they don't taste so bad if they are really, really cold, especially if you're really, really hot and thirsty. Now, what does that remind you of? Right, commercial American beer.

As all the grocery store owners will tell you, beer drinkers are the same people buying wine coolers. Of course, those macho guys don't drink the sissy stuff. No, they buy it for their girlfriends.

Another thing you learn in the detective business is to take your leads where you find them. I found myself at home talking to Jakelyn about my trip. Just for the heck of it, I asked her about wine coolers. Jakelyn says that everyone in her high school drinks wine coolers at the huge parties held at their parents' houses when their parents go out of town. Jakelyn went to her room with a sly smile on her face.

I waited a few minutes, and went down to rummage through the garbage. It must have been a hell of a party. Four trash cans were filled with empty beer cans and dozens of wine cooler bottles. I grabbed my keys and rushed to the wine cellar. It was untouched. I selected an old pinot noir and went up to the porch to ponder my leads.

I concluded the following:

1) Wine coolers are an innocuous, quaffable beverage that, when taken in large amounts, will give you a buzz.

2) People drinking wine coolers are not the same people drinking fine wines.

3) For the most part, people drinking wine coolers have no past history of wine appreciation at all.

4) If all of those people currently drinking wine coolers ever decide to move on to fine wines, there won't be enough good wine to supply them with drink for even one of their more sedate parties.

Hmmm. Jake, I believe you're onto something here.

Let's forget about wine coolers. Let's get back to a sense of humor. Bartles and Jaymes are funny. Their product must be fun. That guy Bruce Willis is crazy on the "Moonlighting" TV show. Now he's crazy on Seagrams wine cooler commercials. No one who's crazy can be serious. That product must be fun. California Cooler is surfing and wipe-outs and girls in bikinis. Must be fun, right?

Not only is it fun, but it's *UN*sophisticated. It's modern. It's MTV video hipness. It's no different from Coke or Pepsi. It's just another American beverage. And it's selling millions and millions of cases to millions and millions of people who don't know how to take a cork out of a bottle.

What if one of the big boys, say Gallo or Seagrams or even Almaden, stopped trying to make their jug wines sound so sophisticated? What if one of the big guys made their jug wines sound like...fun? What if they got away from medals and classical music and soft lighting, and went to some ass-kicking, super slick, rock'n roll videos to sell their jug wine?

What if Bruce Willis filled a Bartles and Jaymes wine cooler bottle with Taylor California Cellars chablis and 7-up, and Bartles and Jaymes couldn't tell the difference? What if Bartles and Jaymes said that sometimes they just like to sit on their porch and drink good old jug wine?

What if good old jug wine becomes just one more great American beverage like Coke or Pepsi or wine coolers?

The implications boggle the mind. Wine at every party. Wine on every table. Wine with every meal. Wine being treated just like any other great beverage, just like it is in most of the civilized world.

Get the public to drink wine as a regular, good-time beverage, and they will move themselves on up, drinking every last drop of white zinfandel as well as every bottle of cabernet sauvignon, chardonnay, pinot noir, and sauvignon blanc.

Get just one of the big boys to pursue what's staring them in the face. Get just one to make wine fun, and then stand back and watch the rest scramble.

It's only a matter of time before one of the big boys tries it. They have an incentive, and the incentive is money...lots of it. If they're making money on coolers, imagine how much they can make on jug wine.

Listen, big boys, go for it. It will make you rich beyond your wildest dreams, and it will drag the rest of the industry along on your coattails. Do your own research, but remember you heard it here first.

And I thank you for your kind support.

FOOD FOR THOUGHT

My face was sweating. My throat was raw. I kept
trying to stop, but I couldn't. I certainly didn't need any
more, but I had to have another little taste. I knew I'd feel
terrible later. It didn't matter. One more and I'd call it
quits. "One more, Chuy, if I can fit it in."

Chuy grabbed a handful of his thinly sliced beef
strips. They had been soaking in his special marinade
overnight. He tossed them on top of the sizzling griddle.
He added chopped onions and freshly chopped cilantro.
As he used the broad spatula to move and turn the meat,
he gave it a few shakes of his house blend of peppers and
salts. He piled the meat on two steaming hot, freshly
made corn tortillas. He hit the taco with two large spoon-
fuls of Palace hot sauce made from jalapeno, serrano *and*
habanero chilies, and he set the miracle that is a Palace
Taco in front of me.

"That makes six, amigo. Want another cerveza,
tambien?"

I nodded yes, and started in on the taco. The flavors
exploded in my mouth, rich and delicious. Then like a
stream of molten lava, the heat and flavor of the chilies
flowed over my tongue and lips. Tears formed in my
eyes, blurring the sign on Chuy's wall that read, "El mas
macho llora aqui," which roughly translates as "Even the
strongest of men cry here."

Chuy had a theory about hot sauce. He felt that the
special chili oils that created the heat changed their chemical make-up upon mixing with saliva. This new chemical
compound short-circuited the communication between the

brain and the stomach. So, even when the stomach is shouting to the brain, "Hey, that's enough, I'm full," that message is being overridden by the tastebuds in the mouth which are shouting, "Just a little bit more, come on, what's it going to hurt?"

Chemistry remains a mystery to Jake Lorenzo. It doesn't matter if it's chile oils, tannins in wine, or cream of tartar in egg whites. I can't really get a handle on it.

That's why I was going to see Dr. Iggy Calamari. *The San Francisco Chronicle* had run some unintelligible article about lead in wine. They made it sound like people were going to suffer some horrible consequences if they drank wine. I figured I'd better check it out for myself.

Iggy Calamari is a long time friend of mine. He invented the wine powered pace maker. He tried to get me and Robert Parker to do a wine review show on public television, but that project fell through. He now works for the wine industry as a researcher.

We sat at his lab counter sipping a Berthoud Zinfandel and Iggy explained. "Jake, this whole lead thing is bogus. We've been testing California wines for years. They average about 25 parts per billion. Per billion, Jake. Believe me, that's not much.

"Hell, the EPA standard for drinking water is 50 ppb, and that's based on the consumption of 1/2 gallon of water per day over a 70 year period. Who drinks that much wine for that long a period of time? No one, that's who.

"Not only that, but when we do have problems with lead content, children and infants turn out to be the most susceptible. Generally, they are not in the wine drinking population."

I sipped my wine, "Come on, Iggy, there's got to be something to this. Why are they testing for lead in the first place?"

"I'm telling you the truth, Jake. In my opinion this whole thing is bogus. It's probably more harrassment from the neo-prohibitionists. Wine averages 25 ppb lead content. Fresh spinach averages 55, french fries 60, and canned tuna 168. Nearly all foods contain traces of lead, and *traces* is all they contain."

"Well, what about these lead capsules?" I ask. "I keep hearing how they are outlawing those."

"Jake, it is true that the tin-lead capsule can impart some minute amounts of lead to the wine that passes over it, but if you cut the foil below the bead and wipe the top of the bottle with a clean damp cloth, that will take care of it."

Iggy got up, went to his desk and got a pile of papers. He brought them over and tossed them on the counter. The title read, "A Little Lead Can Be Good" by Dr. Iggy Calamari.

Iggy put on his most doctoral expression and said, "Remember Jake, things interact in the world of science. They are not good or bad. They are both positive and negative at the same time.

"Now, Jake, you must understand that I am a theoretician. I don't do pure research per se. I do not have proven results. I'll leave that to the FDA and other groups, but my research leads to some interesting conclusions.

"The planet is suffering great stress to its atmosphere. The ozone layer is being depleted at far too rapid a pace. This allows more of the sun's ultraviolet radiation to reach the earth."

"I've read about that," I said. "They're advising everyone to forget about tans and to use sun block when they are outdoors."

"Exactly, Jake, nature and evolution have a way of balancing things. What if the population is picking up

114

small, minute quantities of lead and ingesting them into their systems at exactly the same time as this increase of radiation is reaching the earth? Wouldn't the lead in a person's body act just like a lead shield to protect the system from the harmful rays?"

"You mean like when you get an X-ray?" I asked.

"Sure," said Iggy. "It could happen. I've also uncovered evidence that suggests that as the millions of lead capsules oxidize in our humid bay area atmosphere, they contribute infinitesimal amounts of complex chemical compounds to the atmosphere. These complex compounds are the secret to maintaining the special character of the yeasts that make our famous sourdough French breads."

"So you're telling me that if I keep drinking wine I'll be able to get myself a good tan and eat lots of great French bread."

Iggy shook his head. "I'm telling you that minute amounts of lead in your system are normal and that there may be some positive aspects to it. You can drink 1/2 gallon of water a day for 70 years. You can go to a diet of canned tuna fish. Or you can drink a little wine every day. You make the choice."

The good doctor and I talked for quite some time. He knows a hell of a lot about lead. He reminded me that men have long hoped for a little lead in their pencil. He's even working on a method that concentrates the build up of lead into your fingernails. That way you could write with your finger, and you wouldn't need a pencil. He says he's close on that one, but he doesn't know where to put the erasers.

Of course, I've known Dr. Calamari for a lot of years. You can't believe everything he tells you. On the other hand, he's always food for thought, and I don't think there's any lead in that.

WINE INDUSTRY
SURVIVAL GUIDE

On a beautiful spring day, not too long ago, Jake
Lorenzo was in the heartland of America for the Cincin-
nati International Wine Festival. He had been hired as an
expert in International Wine Security. Jake found himself
seated on a prestigious panel addressing the "State of
Wine in the 90's."

As one winemaker after another addressed more
than 60 attendees, Jake sat quietly, politely doodling on a
piece of paper on the table in front of him. He listened to
winemakers decry the intrusion of the governmental
agencies into their business, listened to them moan about
tin-lead capsules and the new prohibitionism. He heard
them complain about the chardonnay-cabernet world and
predict an "ABC" (anything but chardonnay) world for
the 90's.

He listened while winemakers talked about the
healthful aspects of wine, explained the new organic
growing methods, and described wonderful combinations
of food and wine. It occurred to Jake Lorenzo that wine in
the 90's was going to be serious, expensive business, and
as he sat there, Jake decided he wanted no part of it.

When Jake got his turn to speak, he presented for
the first time his comprehensive "Wine Industry Survival
Guide for the 90's." Here is a short review.

PART I: DEFEND YOUR CASTLE
The wine industry is under attack. It took you a
long time to figure it out, but by now most of you have

caught on. The first thing to do in any war is to secure the homefront.

Jake Lorenzo advises stockpiling a strong private cellar. Buy now, while it's still legal. Put the wine in cool, dark surroundings. Stash bottles all over your house and grounds. Bury age worthy reds in your yard like land mines. When the enemy overruns your house, when the government intrudes into your dining room, when drinking wine is no longer allowed in public, be sure you still have access.

The good soldier must think of himself first. Only then will he be an effective fighter against the enemy.

No wine drinker can fight the good fight if he is deprived of his vinous sustenance. Be sure you have enough on hand for yourself, your loved ones, and your fellow comrades of the cork.

PART II: SUBVERSION AND INCURSION

The best defense is a good offense. The enemy has been allowed to advance uncontested for too long. We're in no position for a confrontation. Once we've secured a sound defensive position; attack.

Guerrilla activity is the way to go. Stick and move. Get in, get out. Win the hearts of the common man, and soon you'll have won the war.

The wine industry needs to quit talking to the already converted, and reach out to the common man. Johnny Appleseed has been and gone. It's time for a Johnny Grapeseed. Better yet, a Jake Grapeseed.

Use some humor, and tell people about the simple joy of wine. Let them see the excitement of production, and the natural goodwill of the people who grow the grapes and make the wine. Teach them that winemaking is farming -- natural and good for the environment.

117

Remind them that one of the main ingredients in the magical elixir of wine is alcohol. Take pride in its ability to reduce stress, make us laugh, help us have a good time, but don't make it sound like medicine. People don't need to get healthier, they need to get happier.

PART III: CLEAN THE NEST

The wine industry has been infiltrated. The enemy has intruded so completely into our industry, that we no longer recognize them.

Wine is not million dollar chateaus, $40 bottles, and triple markups in restaurants. Wine was never meant to be an ass-kissing contest to see who can get the most points or the most medals. We shouldn't be agreeing to ways to lower the amount of wine people drink (i.e. drink less, but drink better.)

We need to reach the common man. Get good wine at a fair price. Let people go to a restaurant where they can have a $10 lunch and a $15 bottle of good wine. As an industry we must encourage restaurants to offer good, lower-priced wines. Jake Lorenzo is sick of seeing nothing but iced tea served at America's lunch table. Pay attention. The people have spoken. They aren't going to pay $30 for a bottle of wine at lunch.

Let's remind the wine shop owners that they must seek out the good values, special wines at reasonable prices. They can continue to sell the high scoring, high-priced wines to the suckers who must have them, but for the future of the industry, we must awaken the people to the joys of wine. The people are having a tough time. They need good $6-10 wine.

PART IV: SHARE

Talk to everyone. Give people wine. Plumber working at the house, give him a bottle. Painter touching up the trim; give him a bottle. Doctor checking out the kids, give him a bottle. Give bottles to the grocery clerks, the person behind the deli counter, your barber, the trash collector.

Let the people in on the secret, and don't treat them like idiots. The working man and woman can't afford to spend a lot of money on wine. Offer them special prices at the winery. Entice the restaurants around town to offer special deals. Consider them "loss leaders" to get people into the store.

It's simple. Keep your powder dry. Have a corkscrew on hand at all times. Get off your high horse and drink with the fella next door.

COMPUTERS

With this column, Jake Lorenzo pops his cherry. That's right, for the first time you are reading a Jake Lorenzo column created on a computer,

I'm sure this comes as a big shock for all of you sophisticated wine types who seem to have been born with computers. I remember being in a very large winery last year. I was waiting to take the winemaker to a baseball game. I was in a warm carpeted room with several computer terminals buzzing away atop very modern, fancy desks.

Well, you know Jake, always the garrulous type. I asked one of the computer operators what his job was. "Assistant winemaker," was his reply.

"What are you doing?"

"I'm doing a blend."

Trust me, this guy has never had wine-stained fingers. He's never had the cellar chill seep down into the marrow of his bones until only an early morning Irish coffee could thaw it out. This guy has never even thought about buying a pair of rubber boots, but this son of a bitch really thought that he was making wine. He worked it out on his computer. Let some poor, cold, dumb cellar rat hook up the hoses, clean the tank, gas it and make sure it's topped. If the idiot can just follow the printed instructions, the wine will be perfect.

Believe me, it was an experience that chilled Jake Lorenzo to the bone. Of course, I used the experience to force the winemaker to pay for all the beers at the ballgame by threatening to reveal his sordid winemaking practices.

Actually, I've always been fond of computers. In fact, way back when I was a teenager, I worked for my uncle's data processing company. I worked with this great guy named Benny. We were burster operators.

In those days everything that a computer printed rolled through on computer paper, even paychecks. The burster was the machine that tore the sheets and then stacked them in order. The main requirement for being a burster operator, at least as far as my mentor Benny was concerned, was to be able to cuss like hell in several different languages every time the burster stopped tearing the pages in the right place and started eating the reports that all these high paid programmers were waiting for in their nice, warm, carpeted offices.

Smart programmers would be very nice to Benny and me. They would bring us a beer now and then. They would get us one of the company tickets to ballgames. Occasionally, they'd let us go with them to the bars where they always picked up the tab.

The other programmers were always having trouble with their reports. Pages were constantly getting chewed up by the burster, or the burster would stack their pages out of sequence, or the payroll checks for their big account with the 2,000 employees would somehow have huge chunks torn out by the terrible burster. Of course, they were all high paid computer programmers sitting in their warm carpeted offices, and they certainly couldn't concern themselves with those poor, dumb burster operators.

Is there a moral to this story? No doubt, but what I was getting at was I've decided to use computers at this late date, because I'm convinced that the technology has progressed to the point where it *won't* change my life.

Computers are so sophisticated that I don't need to know anything about them. I just get my friendly computer guy to load the program, show me how to work it, and I'm off.

I've learned it doesn't matter how proficient you are at one thing, when you get started on something new, you tend to have no confidence in your ability to succeed. I suppose that's why my uncle, who is now retired, called me to ask about setting up a wine cellar for his grandchildren.

Setting up a cellar for children is a commendable practice, and Jake Lorenzo certainly wants to encourage more people to set them up. However, I'm convinced that most people are going about this all wrong.

Most people buy a bunch of great wine from the birth year vintage of their child (or grandchild.) Then they sit around for 21 years waiting for the kid to come of age so they can lay all this wine on him. I would assume that most of the wine has gone bad, so the kid's first experience with fine wine is anything but enjoyable.

Jake Lorenzo has a much more sensible program. Go ahead and buy the wine from the kid's birth year, but as soon as the kid is able to reason, take him down and show him all those bottles. Let him touch them. Let him look at the labels. Explain that all of this will someday be his. When the kid is a teenager and screws up--you know, stays out too late or flunks computer class--take him down to the cellar. Pick out one of his bottles of wine. Open it and drink it in front of him. Tell him how good it is and what a shame it is that he'll never get a chance to know how good it is.

This will teach your kid about the true value of wine. He'll be able to watch the real pleasure you get from drinking a fine bottle. This way the wine cellar becomes a valuable educational tool. Believe me, that kid will treasure any of the bottles that might be left when he gets to 21.

By the way, I'd like to enlist your help for a friend of mine. His name is Kieran Toovey. He's a little more than 2 years old. He's talking pretty good now, although most of what he has to say seems to come from Mutant Ninja Turtles or Disney's The Mermaid.

Kieran's dad was Tracy Toovey who was murdered by Ramon Salcido in April, 1989. Kieran isn't going to remember his dad. He was too young when Tracy was killed. I thought it might be a nice gesture if those of us in the wine business built a cellar for Kieran.

Kieran's birth year was 1988. As you release your 1988's, what do you say you send a bottle or two to Cathy Toovey for "Kieran's Cellar." I think Kieran will be impressed when he gets older to see how many wineries have sent bottles in honor of Tracy. He still won't know his father, but he will know that a lot of us thought Tracy was a hell of a guy.

If nothing else, I know you'll be doing Cathy a favor. If I'm any judge of character, Kieran's going to have her down in the cellar often, watching as she drinks one of his bottles and explains how good it would have been.

LETTERS IN

Dear Jake:

I've been reading your stuff in *"Practical Winery"* now for years. I've always enjoyed your writing immensely, but the "Welcome Companion" article hit home.

I live here in the Mother Lode where there is still a "thread" of pioneer spirit and a chance for those of us who are "unique" to live the good life outside the "mainstream."

I began making wine in the '70's; my passion for the grape led me to bond my own winery in 1986. I knew it wouldn't be easy-- you see, I was born without... a silver spoon. But, I was convinced my talent and this passion I had for the art of winemaking would prevail.

It's now 1992. I just spent $7,000 on new foil capsules *without* lead, that despicable killer of oenophiles. The Feds want $1,000 by July 1. It's a "special tax" on top of the tax I pay per gallon. The State has increased its tax per gallon--after all, there is a budget deficit. No insurance company in its right "corporate" mind would bond this tiny operation. All the local bankers laugh when I ask for a loan secured by all those weird looking tanks, barrels, and winery equipment.

The cost of labels (with all the required warnings to save pregnant women, etc.), glass and corks also keep going up, up, up... and oak... I think you covered it well in your article. I could go on. Pop one of these suckers; I think you'll like my product.

It's not only the current hard economic times, Jake. It's the erosion of the "pioneer spirit"--tax, regulate into oblivion, charge what the "traffic will bear" for supplies, equipment, etc. Sebastiani, Mondavi and the ancient family-based can afford it. The Japanese and foreign owned wine conglomerates can afford it. Who the hell will miss my 2,500 cases of wine?

I'm thinking about giving up, Jake. I'm 42 and I'm tired. I love the hard work in the cellar at the winery. But the bureaucratic bullshit and the hard economic times are making me tired and breaking that "spirit" I once had. I just don't seem to have the same passion I once had for this "business." I wake up in a sweat now because I owe the bank $30,000...I don't have. I wonder in '92 if I made a big mistake chasing a "pipe dream" back in the '70's. That's what my ex-wife thinks. They *are* hard economic times--I think I could weather that storm. But there's *more*. I won't even discuss such "subtle" things like the neo-prohibitionist movement. I'm tired, Jake. Perhaps there's room for another guy in your new endeavor.

Enter Richard Matranga, welcome companion... Richard Matranga is a charming scallywag. He's a first rate musician, well versed in legal matters and makes one "shit-kicking Port wine." Funny too. Now available to help you enjoy all that expensive crap you've been work-ing so hard to acquire...

Great concept, Jake! But you'd probably have to obtain a city business license and pay a State franchise tax; the attorney general would scrutinize such a business for misleading claims, you know. The IRS would surely tax you on such obvious benefits. Before long, you'd prob-ably be worried about the overhead too.

Regards,
Richard Matranga /s/
Sonora Port Works

125

LETTERS OUT

Dear Richard:

Thanks for the Port and for the contribution to
Kieran's Cellar. Thanks also for your passionate letter.
You have paid Jake Lorenzo the ultimate writer's compliment by taking the time to write in response to my column.

I've been writing for quite some time about exactly
the kinds of things you describe in your letter. As you
have recognized, I share your passion and frustration.

Jake Lorenzo's got no advice to give anyone. Hell,
it's hard enough trying to advise myself. Personally, I've
learned this about the wine business: I've always loved
wine, and I always will. I've never cared much for business, and I'm not going to start now.

For me, wine is art. It has the power to transport us
to a higher plane. It empowers us with visions of possibilities. It is different in each and every encounter. It is different for each one of us. It resists definition and quantifica-
tion. It is eternal. People will always make wine, just as
people will always write, sing and paint.

Business is based on profit, not a bad thing, in and
of itself. Unfortunately, profit (and therefore business) is
selfish. Sooner or later-- when the shit hits the fan, when
the economy goes into the dumper, when push comes to
shove-- business acts to save itself.

I've heard business justify doing some pretty
despicable things by saying that it must to survive. Business people make the argument that if their business

doesn't survive, then they will be unable to do beneficial works later on.

Jake's law of life reads, "For every thing gained, something was sacrificed." (This is certainly the law of winemaking.)

If you must do something despicable to survive, then you will forever be a little despicable yourself. Make a few despicable sacrifices in a row and you'll never get back to where you thought you were headed. You may gain survival, but you risk sacrificing the dream.

Richard, you mention the "erosion of pioneer spirit."

There is no such thing. A pioneer is the person who goes first, or does something first, and so prepares the way for others to follow. We can't all be pioneers.

Pioneers are imbued with the artistic sensibility. It is the visionary artistic sense that allows them to risk being first. The exhilaration of discovery is a powerful stimulant, and the joy and well being provided by that stimulant cries out to be shared.

Imagine the disappointment of the pioneer who discovers that no one wants to follow, that no one wants to share in the dream, that, in fact, people have no idea what the hell the dream is.

We can't all be pioneers, too few of us have the stomach for it.

Richard, we have never met, but I doubt that you are losing your passion, or that you risk losing your spirit. Rather, I think you have a flu, the business flu.

I think you have that artistic sensibility, and it is speaking to you now. It is telling you that business is selfish where you are not. It is telling you that the dream was yours, and belongs not to others. It is reminding you to take joy in your own process of creation, and to remember that no one else can share the exhilaration of your own personal pioneering.

We can't all be pioneers. We can be artists.

I know one thing for sure, Jake Lorenzo's got no business worth being despicable, and I'm always going to be artist enough to enjoy a good bottle of wine, or port.

Keep drinking, and keep in touch.

Sincerely,

Jake /s/

PART IV

Travels
and
Travails

BRUNO

We saw the first one at Brolio castle. He opened the heavy metal gate and waved us through. Obviously a working man, with clothes dirty from the good earth. His hands were gnarled, his hair gray, his face weathered. He was that classic Tuscan age, somewhere between 50 and 1,000. Hard to tell.

We called him Bruno. Look around and Bruno's gone. We wander down to the chapel. The door swings open. Bruno stands to the side with downcast eyes. Glance at the stained glass and we're alone. We walk through the gardens. Bruno appears to calm the dogs. Take a right to the castle, and from the inside, the doors slowly open, Bruno in the wings.

Every castle and badia has a Bruno. Ancient, unspeaking, lightning fast. Able to pass through walls. Always ahead of you, never where you last saw him.

Take it from Jake Lorenzo, the Brunos of Tuscany are the missing links to her past. Keepers of the castle, mute remnants of the feudal times. Bruno may have secrets, but he ain't talking.

Tuscany is a land of startling hard beauty. I remember the stunning glory of the Tuscan hills with ancient badias and towers guarding the grapevines and olive trees, just as they have for more than 1,000 years. I also remember the incongruity of the sun glinting off stainless steel tanks nestled into the battle-scarred walls of antiquity.

Mostly, I remember the people, hard and gnarled like the hills. Provincial thinkers, perfectly satisfied with Tuscan wine, unsalted Tuscan bread, Tuscan pasta and steak fiorentina. Not in the least curious about other peoples, their foods or their lives. Tuscans are old, somewhere between 50 and 1,000, hard to tell.

Jake Lorenzo has to wonder, 'Where the hell are the kids?"

Screaming through the streets of Firenze on their pestilential motor scooters is my guess.

Kids have curiosity, and it must be satisfied. So they move to the cities, go to school, watch MTV. They become Italian lawyers and accountants and bankers. They live in crowded, noisy cities. They work hard, become successful and prosperous. They buy fashionable clothes, drive fancy, tiny cars, and furnish lovely apartments.

They give up leisurely meals in simple country restaurants to wolf down panini standing in crowded bars. They give up 60 minute cappuccinos at an outside table for a gulped espresso standing in a packed shop. They develop stress and tension, and when they make their rare trips home to the countryside, they find that the land prices have tripled, housing has quadrupled.

But the land is unchanged; vines and olive trees, bumpy dirt roads. A slow, unhurried life filled with neighborly gossip.

Who knows when it will hit them. Eventually, it must.

They'll go back to the land. When they do, Bruno will open the doors. He'll show them how to make the wine, how to press the olive oil, but he ain't gonna tell them a damn thing. Let them figure it out for themselves.

It's the Tuscan way.

FREEWAY PAINTING

The chill of dawn made me shiver. Roaring down Highway 101 in the bed of the Ford pickup, I took a long pull at the Hornitos bottle. The wind ripped around the cab and sent Paraquat's paint-spattered shirt flapping.

Paraquat's eyes leaked long tears as the wind tore at his face. "Exactly 50," he screamed. Liz smiled back at us from the cab of the truck, but I don't think she heard.

The bed of the truck contained boxes, each box a different color, each filled with similar colored balloons, each balloon filled with similar colored paint. The boxes were almost empty.

This would be the fourth and final pass. "Get ready," yelled Paraquat as the first glint of morning sun lit upon his mad, ecstatic paint-smeared face.

We were there.

In a frenzy of motion, Paraquat grabbed at the balloons and threw them out of the truck. "More green," he shouted. I threw balloons for all I was worth, but I couldn't match him. In less than two minutes, it was over.

Liz eased off the freeway and expertly wove her way through the winding hillside roads. Paraquat couldn't keep still. He kept jumping up and down like a guy who had to take a leak. "It's gonna be great. It's gonna be great."

The sun behind us, we came around a bend. From high above, we looked out over the freeway and to the ocean beyond. It was great. Plainly, simply, wondrously great. For one short mile, the long, ugly black ribbon that was Highway 101 sparkled with color.

The balloons landed and then exploded, sending paint splattering in all directions. The occasional cars would drive their way through like so many palette knives on a canvas. The Pacific Ocean crashed its waves in applause.

Paraquat Parducci, freeway artist extraordinaire, stopped hugging his lowly assistant, Jake Lorenzo, and jumped down from the truck to plant a wildly satisfied kiss on the lips of his love and inspiration (not to mention his driver) Liz Parducci.

The champagne cork exploded. We drank slowly, watching the ever changing painting until, finally, it had dried.

"Finished," sighed Paraquat.

"The champagne too," added Liz.

"And it's great," I smiled.

That was fifteen years ago.

I have great respect for artists. Not so much for what they actually produce, but for those glorious, ecstatic moments when they are obsessed with the mindless madness of creativity. Artists live for those rare moments, and it is the heartfelt joy "of the moment" that links the artist to the finished work.

The rest of us see only the finished work. We lose sight of the source. We forget that, for the artist, the joy is in the doing. While he may take great pride in the finished product, he realizes it's not much more than a photograph of a place he's been. No more than a faded reminder of some long ago, wonderful trip.

When we talk to an artist about his work, when we tell him how marvelous it is, how it moves us, and how much it means to us, we make him uncomfortable. He's thinking, "I wish you could have been there. I wish you could have seen the real thing. I wish you could share the joy."

134

It is the bane of the artist that all he has to show for the glory of his inspiration is what, for him, must surely pale by comparison. The rest of us are fortunate in that we can take great joy in the creation, whether it be a book, a painting or a bottle of wine.

The only winemaker I know well enough to call friend is Lance Cutler. I have two particular visions in mind. One is of Lance at the 1983 Sonoma County Harvest Fair surrounded by people congratulating him on Gundlach Bundschu's sweepstakes winning wine. He definitely looked uncomfortable.

The other vision is of Lance in a 5,000 gallon tank, face flushed, dripping sweat, shoveling red pomace into the Ministrina. He sticks his head through the manhole for a breath of air, gulps down half the beer I hand him, and says, "It's gonna be great."

The crush can be one ugly black ribbon of long hours and drudgery. Don't forget to notice the splashes of color. Take pause to listen to the explosions of balloons. Take joy in those rare moments of mindless madness.

As for me, I'm taking Jakelyn for a family outing. We're joining Paraquat and Liz just south of Santa Nella on Highway 5. Paraquat has a truck with 500 gallons of bright yellow paint, and in a moment of inspired madness has decided to let it drip out in one long, unending line all the way to Bakersfield.

FREE AMERICA

The windows in Chuy's Burrito Palace were steamy. Condensation ran down in rivulets and collected in tiny puddles on the sill. The smell of frying chorizo filled the air. Like a bear after a long hibernation, I shook out of my coat and sat on my stool, Jake's stool, waiting.

Chuy banged through the swinging kitchen doors, a steaming plate in each hand, did a cha-cha pirouette whistling La Bamba, and dropped both dishes with a crash when he saw me.

Shock melted from his face as a long, slow grin spread from ear to ear. Ignoring the broken crockery, and deftly stepping through the eggs, he danced over to the coffee and poured two cups. Putting them down in front of me, he reached under the counter and brought up the bottle of Hornitos. A hefty shot went into each cup.

"Four months, amigo," he said, "I thought you were dead."

"Sorry, Chuy, I got lost in Free America."

Chuy nodded, then smiled again. He resumed La Bamba and started cleaning up the mess, interrupting only to yell in Spanish at the two complaining customers that if they didn't feel like waiting, then their impatience must be genetically linked to the rapidity with which their fathers had performed the act that conceived them.

Spanish is such a romantic language.

Free America was one of Chuy's discoveries. He had gone to New Orleans for Mardi Gras, and had stayed through Jazz Fest. Of course, a lot of that had to do with a lovely young Southern belle who found Chuy's accent unbelievably erotic. Chuy felt that New Orleans was the last bastion of tolerance in these United States.

American drinkers no longer live in the land of the free. Not only is it a sin to drink and drive, but merely taking a drink now carries a stigma.

Try to buy a beer at an A's baseball game. Not only do they force fans to miss large portions of the game while waiting in long lines for a beer, but they insist on humiliating you, by forcing you to show ID, no matter how old you are.

Heaven protect us from those trying to protect us from ourselves.

New Orleans is drinkers' heaven on earth. It's the land of drive-through frozen daiquiris. It's a town where it's still legal to drink a beer in your car. Drinking on the streets is fine, as long as your beverage is in a "go cup."

In California, when someone has too much to drink and gets a little wild, he can expect recriminations from all his friends the next day. "Boy, did you tie one on. Maybe you should go to a de-tox center. How can you live with what you did?"

They completely ignore the fact that in all likelihood, the guilty party doesn't remember what he did anyway. That's why a New Orleanian will simply say, "You certainly enjoyed yourself last night," or "You were having a great time."

In New Orleans, every person has equal rights. It's a unique concept. The smoker has the same rights as the non-smoker. The drinker has the same rights as the teetotaler. The tourist has the same rights as the locals. (But the locals ain't about to wait in line at K-Paul's when they can eat better, nicer, cheaper, with fine wine at plenty of other restaurants.)

New Orleans understands the concept of voting with your dollars. If they like something, they go there and spend their money. If things don't live up to their standards, they don't go back. Nor do they mourn that business' eventual demise.

New Orleans has an attitude that exists nowhere else in America. (In fact, the only other place it ever existed in America was in draft boards toward the end of the Vietnam War.) Nothing, absolutely nothing, shocks a New Orleanian. Nothing you do, say, wear or don't wear freaks them out. They may comment on your style, but they don't make judgments.

More than that, New Orleans is a town that likes itself for what it is. People in New Orleans are loyal. It's a real pleasure to sell wine there. Buyers taste the wine, and if they like it, they buy it. They put it on their lists and they sell it, year after year. They enjoy building relation-ships with wine people.

Busy, famous chefs love to stand in their kitchens tasting wine with you. After work, around one or two in the morning, they're more than willing to meet you in a club, hear some music, and drink some wine.

In New Orleans, wine ain't no crime.

The time is right for drinkers to revolt. Wine drink-ers are going to have to lead the way. This is a call to arms. I'm tired of telling people that wine is the beverage of moderation.

Wine is the beverage that goes best with food. If you like to eat good food, then wine is what you should be drinking. If the wine is so good that you just keep drink-ing bottle after bottle, then go ahead on, "cher." Jake Lorenzo likes to see y'all have a good time.

SPRING TRAINING

Superior sits ugly and dusty on a spectacular box canyon plateau. The rock mountain mesa behind Superior thrusts upward into the crystal blue Arizona sky. Even now, you have to blink away the vision of Apache warriors atop the mesa.

To the left as you enter town stands the long, flat mountain of tailings. Excreted from the copper mining process, they sit, an ugly reminder of the town's lifeblood. The copper mine fueled Superior. Men would load themselves into the rusty metal elevators and descend into Arizona hell. They would escape ten hours later, dirty and dehydrated. The Superior copper miner could pound down six beers after his shift and not even get a buzz.

The copper miners were hard, tough, proud men who did their work and earned their pay every day. In the heat and darkness of the pit, they couldn't see that copper pennies were worthless, that telephone companies had abandoned copper wire for fiber optics.

The corporate executives gave the miners seven days notice when they closed the mine. Dumped them, like copper tailings, to sit and rot. Superior died six years ago.

*   *   *

I was in Arizona for spring training. Baseball's idyllic rebirth. Rising like a phoenix from the ashes of the past season, each team convinced that this will be the year.

Spring training was tennis in the mornings, ice-cold beers by the pool at 11 a.m., more beer, peanuts and a hot dog at the game while the best hecklers in the world worked themselves into shape. After an afternoon swim,

139

it was out for a fine, inexpensive steak dinner made great by a vintage bottle brought from Sonoma and served for the ridiculous corkage fee of $2.

Lately, things have changed. The snowbirds have come to settle, ripping out the orange groves to put in their condos, motels, trailer parks, and fast-food restaurants. The games are sell-outs. The hecklers are gone, replaced by drunken college kids. People argue for hot dogs and fight over beers. Another of life's treasures reduced to nothing more than fond memories.

So, instead of going to the Giants' game, I drove the 50 miles from Phoenix to Superior. I met an old friend from a past life and we talked of fond memories. We drove through the tunnel to Oak Flats. We admired the incredible rock formations in the pass and watched them take ghostly shape in the aftermath of a bloody sunset. We ended up in the Triple X Bar at quitting time.

The bar filled up. My friend introduced me to the men of Superior. They remain tough, hard and proud. One after another, we met, spoke, and drank. Beers piled up in front of us five and six deep as new friends bought round after round.

I ended up in a stupor on a stool next to Grr. Grr was a mechanic-- a damn good one he told me several times. He hadn't shaved for a few days. He wore working clothes and boots like a cellar rat. His watch cap was pulled low over his eyes. "I drink beer and whiskey," explained Grr, "but when I'm out to dinner with my lady, I like some wine, some good wine."

The next day, on the ride back to Phoenix, I thought about Superior and Grr and that bottle of wine. If a damn good mechanic in a town as remote as Superior is going to drink wine, if he's going to make the magic in that bottle part of the magic in his life, then the future burns bright for California and the wine industry.

If liquor salesmen (who appear congenitally unable to sell wine) don't catch on soon, then they'll be like the copper miners in Superior. They'll wake up one morning wondering when their pennies became worthless.

If people in Sonoma and Napa and the other rare and great growing regions of the world don't recognize the special life viticulture and winemaking provide, then they are doomed to see condominiums and shopping centers planted in their precious soil. Soon the few vineyards left will be no more than that mountain of copper tailings alongside Superior. Another of life's treasures relegated to fond memory.

Later, sitting by the pool in the hot Arizona sun, sipping on a half pint of Hornitos, I was hit with a vision that made me laugh out loud. In my mind's eye, I see Grr ride into Sonoma dressed as an Apache warrior on a bright white horse. He puts piles of money and sacks of copper pennies in front of greedy businessmen in clown suits. He buys the McDonald's and has it torn down. Grr says, "This land is too valuable to plant fast-food restaurants. This land was meant for grapes."

Grr, I like your style.

POLITICS

Here it is 1988, an election year.

I ran for office once. I won, too. I was elected class treasurer of my elementary school in the sixth grade. My campaign speech won it for me.

"I admit I don't have the best mathematical mind. I don't know algebra, and when I do my math I need a pencil with a good eraser. But since the class treasury now has a total of $2.47, I feel well qualified for the job."

It was a dramatic speech, what with the background singers and all, but you had to be there to appreciate its full impact. In any case, it brought them out to the polls. That, and the fact that I ran unopposed, got me elected.

When I moved to Sonoma, one of the first things I learned was: never, ever, under any circumstances, no matter how drunk, should you get into a political discussion with a local.

It is one of the rules by which Jake Lorenzo abides, and over the last 20 years it has saved me considerable anguish. So, please understand that this is not about politics. Don't be sending out the presshounds to dig up skeletons in my closet. Jake Lorenzo is not running for anything.

However, it has occurred to me that America has, in the past, been more confident. I think back to the pioneers moving across the spectacular, fearsome west unbowed by hardship. I think of the Americans fighting in two world wars convinced of their prowess. I remember the peace corps sending our young around the world full of naivete and good will.

142

For more than a century, Americans have been friendly, open, brash and cocky. We thought we were the best, and we went into the world with open-hearted confidence.

It didn't sit too well with the rest of the world. Europeans couldn't handle our casual openness. In a land of class differences, where even today bosses and employees don't socialize, they don't know what to do with Americans who worked and played together.

In Asia, with their structured and codified society, there was no understanding, let alone appreciation, of our wit and friendly intentioned sarcasm. The third world jealously envied our wealth. The entire planet had no idea what American women were up to, and thought American men were wimps for allowing them to do it.

Somehow, all this disapproval, along with Watergate, the Vietnam debacle and a decade of assassinations, made us lose our confidence, our cockiness and our pride. We have given up on things American, and look elsewhere for products, as well as inspiration.

I have just returned from France. My first trip to Europe in 15 years. The French are a fiercely proud people. They believe in things French and they support those things with their francs. Their wines are fantastic, their vineyards stunningly beautiful and their food sublime.

I stood in Alsace, in freezing temperatures, and watched them harvest. I wandered through ancient Burgundian vineyards tasting the world's most famous grapes. I observed and joined the people in their joyous daily consumption of food and wine.

I learned that there is no France without fine food and wine. Nor could there be "French wine" without the long, regional tradition and history of France. In short, French wines themselves are exact expressions of the

143

French way of life. They differ region by region, because the people differ region by region.

There is a secret to be learned here. If we presume to make great wines in California and elsewhere in America, then those wines must reflect a uniquely American spirit. If wine is ever to be a part of our daily lives, then those wines must reflect and represent the way we live.

It seems simple enough, but, somehow, we've missed it. I mean, is America a bunch of snobs in black tie sniffing at glasses, or is it a bunch of friends slamming down some zinfandel along with big plates of spaghetti?

We do not have a long proud history of viticulture and winemaking like the French, Nor are we, like the French, bound to ancient and archaic rules and customs.

Those of us working in the wine industry have a unique opportunity. We have a chance to shape and mold what will surely become a glorious and successful history of our own. Let's not copy someone else's version. Let us, instead, be open to new ideas, brash about exploring uncharted arenas, and confident in our ability to succeed.

It's what America once was. It's what we can be again. I'll tell you this, Jake Lorenzo would give up Hornitos to see it happen in my lifetime.

AT THE WINERY

The Sonoma fog rises eerily. My jet black steed glistens, eyes blazing, as he charges ahead. Up in the saddle, straining forward, I reach out.

All of us are trying for the brass ring when it is offered. Private eyes are no different.

It began this way.

Chuy's Burrito Palace sizzles with the pungent aroma of chorizo and eggs. Chuy slams the plate down on top of the airplane ticket. He pours a dollop of Hornitos into my coffee and takes a slug from the bottle for himself.

"What's the big deal, carnal? So I buy my amigo a plane ticket. Four months, you ain't done nothing. Even when I get you an easy money trabajo, you drop out on me."

He's right. I mean, I'm a private eye. It's what I do for a living. Chuy had me lined up for two weeks security work for a local rock star. Easy money for sure, but I just couldn't face another group of 35 year old heavy metal rock stars with their adolescent "party till you drop" mentality.

"You got people all over asking for you, but you don't do nothing."

Chuy's right again. Even now, letters from the Epicurean, Wine and Spirits, and Montelle Notes sit unanswered. To hell with Crocodile Dundee, they say. Australia wants Jake Lorenzo. Offers of fantastic debauchery Down Under. Promises of readers eager for my insights, charmed by my wit. Even apologies for their weakened dollar, as they promise exorbitant payment for

145

my columns. But I haven't even done my columns for
PMV, let alone all the others.

"Hey, amigo, look at it as a loan. I know you're
good for it. Besides, it's worth it so I don't have to look at
your ugly face cada dia."

I take the ticket, and head out. Chuy's grinning.
"Homes, don't let them push you around. Recuerdo, this
dude's on his home turf. Scope it out, watch your back,
then blow him away."

The plane ride to D.C. is uneventful except for the
two desperate dives to avoid other aircraft somewhere
over Utah. I look up from Elmore Leonard in time to
catch the end of the movie. A bunch of chimpanzees stole
a government airplane and took off for monkey paradise.

I get my bag out of Dulles Airport in a speedy 84
minutes, jump into a cab driven by a gentleman who
assures me that he used to be a colonel in the Iranian Air
Force. We get into Georgetown in record time. I walk into
Chadwick's, order a Sam Adams, and haven't finished
half of it, when Dr. Iggy Calamari slaps me on the back.

Iggy is doing splendidly working as a lobbyist for
the Wine Institute. His wine-powered pacemaker is
almost ready for release. In the meantime, he spends his
time drinking fine California wines with influential politicians, all the while extolling wine's medical, life-sustaining
virtues.

We cab it over to the Willard, where we sip wine
with the ghosts of Grant. Then, we hoof it over to the
Occidental for port amongst the 8x10s. We finish with our
own bottle of Hornitos on the steps of Congress.

I love Washington D.C.

The next morning, I sit sweating under the hot TV
lights. Slightly hazy from my evening with the good Dr.
Calamari, I am reminded that D.C. is a city of addicts, and
that the drug of choice is power. In D.C., it's not just

146

whom you know, it's how closely you rub up against them.

In this town of players, Jake Lorenzo, private eye and sometime wine writer, sits in the blinding light waiting for wine writing's supreme commander to take him on. One on one. Mano a mano. Due to Dr. Calamari's sick brainstorm, on behalf of the Wine Institute, we are about to film a test pilot called "At the Winery." It's meant to be a take-off on Siskel and Ebert. On this side, Jake Lorenzo, private eye. Across the bar, the boss, the ultimate player, Robert Parker.

Robert Parker is fun to read. He is opinionated, experienced and well-qualified to do what he does. To my way of thinking, he's the best at rating and describing wines, but you can't read him for too long without all those wines and descriptions running together. I recommend you do what I do. Keep your copy of "The Wine Advocate" in the bathroom, and read him in short spurts.

Robert Parker tastes Bordeaux wines when they are six, nine and eighteen months of age. He tastes them several weeks to a month after assemblage has been completed. He tastes vintage Bordeaux single-blind, using proper glasses, correct temperatures and colored backgrounds. He rates wines with his 100 point system.

Jake Lorenzo doesn't do any of that stuff. I don't taste a chef's raw eggs to determine the future of his souffle, nor would I try Chuy's raw chorizo while he's curing it in the refrigerator. I actually prefer zinfandel served in those jelly jar-like Italian wine glasses, and I will never understand America's need to assign numerical superiority and inferiority to everything. It smacks of grammar school and gold stars, or puffs, or whatever.

Robert Parker seems dedicated to his work. He appears to be a thorough man of great integrity. But, his very system forces us to focus on wine as a commodity.

His writing encourages people to buy wines as investments. While Parker's great experience allows him to understand that, in the proper setting, "a simple wine can become sublime and memorable," too often his writings are used by wine buyers as the exclusive reason for refusing to put those simple wines on their shelves.

In short, it is folly to try to quantify quality, especially in something as vibrant and varied as wine. The attempt to do so, not only denigrates the product itself, it also performs a disservice to those whose very lives are entwined in its production.

I realize Robert Parker is in business. I wish him success, but he shouldn't overlook David Shaw in the *Los Angeles Times*. "On the European continent, most people grow up drinking wine. It is an integral part of their culture. They do not need a writer to tell them what to drink."

Surely, for all of us who love wine, Robert Parker included, making wine an integral part of American culture is an honorable and desired goal. This continual bowing and scraping at the altar of the mythical "best" is self-defeating.

Needless to say, "At the Winery" didn't work out. I knew from the beginning it wouldn't, but there are times in a man's life when he must stand up and be counted. There are times when he must make the grand, futile gesture. I'm Jake Lorenzo, private eye. Making the grand, futile gesture is what I do. It's something I'm good at.

Someday, I'd like to spend an evening with Robert Parker on my home turf. I'd like to take him on a pub crawl around the Sonoma Plaza. We'd run into local growers, winemakers and cellar rats. I'd take him to the Burrito Palace for a late breakfast of chorizo and eggs.

And, if the fog is just right, I'll treat him to a ride on the merry-go-round, and he can have a try at his own brass ring.

YIN AND YANG

I am having a hard time controlling Chuy, not that Chuy is controllable. We are riding in the elevator at McGraw-Hill Publishing Company on our way to a meeting with some executive editor to discuss my book, *Cold Surveillance.*

Chuy, who will shortly be acting as my agent, is lightly bouncing from one foot to the other. "Jake, amigo, did you hear that bonita secretary? 'Yo, take da elavater to da twenty eight flo. Hang a right 'n you dere.' I'm in love, Jake."

Chuy Palacios, graduate of the University of California at Berkeley and owner of the Burrito Palace, says actress Rosie Perez's voice is a powerful sexual stimulant. In the land of New York, full of beautiful Puerto Rican women talking like Rosie Perez, my erstwhile agent is completely unhinged.

We enter the designated office and meet Sofia Rodriguez, editor at McGraw-Hill. Chuy freezes in midstride. Ms. Rodriguez has raven hair, pouty red lips, a shimmering black silk blouse and a short, tight red leather skirt. She says, "It's a pleasure to meetcha. I been hopin' we could do sumthin' wid yo book, cuz I find it very exceptional, very, very exceptional."

Chuy walks slowly to the wall and bangs his head against it three times.

The meeting went downhill from there. I didn't mind, really. I never thought a major publishing house would take on a project like *Cold Surveillance.* I came to New York because I had some business, and because

149

Rusty Staub had invited me to opening day at Shea Stadium.

Chuy came along because he has an abiding passion for the Colorado Rockies ever since they signed Andres Galarraga. Chuy maintains he's the only person in America who can correctly pronounce Andres' name. They also dated sisters for awhile.

On the subway to Shea, a disconsolate Chuy said, "Lo siento, Jake. I don't know what happened. It's just that accent, amigo. I couldn't help myself."

"It's all right, Chuy. If they had decided to publish my book, every agent in New York would have started banging their head against walls to close a deal. You probably saved me from a law suit."

"Just the same, Jake. It's not professional. Cuando yo trabajo para ti, I like to be professional."

"You're way off base, pal. I doubt there's another agent in all of New York who can pound his head against a wall, blow a book deal, and still get a date with the editor. That's professional in my book."

"I guess you're right," said Chuy, brightening a bit. "It's all in how you look at it. C'mon Jake, I'm buying the beers today."

*   *   *

I love New York. There's an electricity that makes your nerve endings stand at attention. Your senses are on red alert. Time speeds up. The trains go fast, so do the cabs. Even stuck in traffic, there's a quivering tension.

New York City is a melange. Every culture on earth is represented, every food, every language. The good, the bad and the ugly coexist on every block, in every bar, in every neighborhood.

150

Life on the street permeates all levels of society in New York. Just as your reputation is everything in the "hood," it is no less so at the top of the social ladder. Who you know, how you do, and what you wear all matter in Manhattan.

Shake hands with a New Yorker and they'll never look you in the eye, because they're too busy checking the room for someone with a bigger rep, more juice, or a flashier gold chain.

New York is about surface. People relate to the facade you give them to view. If you want to succeed in New York, your facade better be a good one. Or unique. Or twisted. Or hilarious, but don't let it be one they've seen before, especially if they've seen it done better.

Like I said, I love New York. After all, who's got a better act than Jake Lorenzo? For Jake Lorenzo, being in New York is ongoing improvisational theater, and it carries the nerve-jangling thrill of living on the edge.

As much as I like excitement, I can only take so much. When New York gets the blood churning like Niagara Falls, when the electric excitement of the place feels like a runaway subway train, when it's time to chill; I go to New Orleans.

If New York is electricity, New Orleans is a valium IV, or at the very least a drive-through daiquiri stand.

You can't be nervous in New Orleans, unless the Saints are in a play-off game. You can't get excited in New Orleans, unless Aaron Neville decides to stand up and sing *a capella* in the laundromat while you're folding your underwear. The only facades in New Orleans are in the French Quarter.

When someone comes on with their "act," New Orleanians smile, say "Is that right, babe?" and order another drink. The only thing New Orleanians have time for is perusing menus at fine restaurants, or reading through Gambit to decide what kind of music to hear that night.

As much as I love New Orleans, there comes a time when I've got to push away from the table. When it's too much trouble to pinch another crawfish tail, when elevated food is making me dizzy, when the beignets harden; I go home to Sonoma.

*   *   *

Sitting in my garden, sipping on some gamay, I hold the .38 revolver lightly, hoping some miserable gopher will try to take off one of my tomato plants. I quietly reflect on my travels. It occurs to me that Napa and Sonoma are much like New York and New Orleans.

Shake hands with a Napa Valley winery owner and watch their eyes dart about. Mention a wine cave, and theirs is deeper. Praise a beautiful chateau, and theirs is finer. Talk about price, and theirs is higher. I enjoy Napa Valley, because I appreciate the "act," especially when it's done well.

Spend time with a Sonoma Valley winery owner, and they'll likely pop a cold beer into your hand while they tell you about the fish they almost caught yesterday. Then they'll have you jump into their dusty pick-up truck to bounce around the vineyard. Mention other farmers, they'll say they're great. Talk about other wineries, they'll tell you they make great wine. Ask a technical question, they'll answer simply with a deprecating humor. I love the Sonoma Valley, because it relaxes me.

It occurs to me that we need variety in our lives; excitement *and* relaxation. I like to visit New York *and* New Orleans. I like to drink wines from Napa *and* Sonoma. It's yin *and* yang.

They say water separates the people of the world while wine unites them. Jake Lorenzo says wine is the beverage you should drink while you're building the bridge.   152

GRAPE SECRETS

Dear Editor:

I am writing this letter on behalf of Jake Lorenzo. Mr. Lorenzo is sitting in a hospital bed, in great pain, and has casts on both arms and one leg. He has ingeniously designed one of the casts so that his gun fits into a plaster groove which allows his finger access to the trigger. He is pointing the gun at me as an inducement to write this letter.

I contracted for Mr. Lorenzo's services on a very private and delicate matter involving some members of my immediate family. Since I am the owner of a famous Napa Valley winery, and do not want to compromise any of the aforementioned family members, Mr. Lorenzo has graciously agreed to maintain my anonymity.

This particular matter required that Mr. Lorenzo spend large amounts of time observing those particular persons employed at my famous winery, as well as those particular members of my immediate family that I suspected of having liaisons.

For this task, Mr. Lorenzo cleverly disguised himself as a gardener. His disguise was fantastic in every detail, and thus gave him total access anywhere in my famous winery. (I would also like to mention that as a result of his gardening, our famous winery has never looked lovelier.)

Since we were in the middle of harvest, and since Mr. Lorenzo has a genuine love and respect for the grape, and since this particular case required huge amounts of observation time, because we never knew when the suspected liaisons might occur, Mr. Lorenzo did some spectacular research on grapes and their behavior.

I was first aware of this research when I saw Mr. Lorenzo behind one of the wine tanks on his hands and knees looking through a magnifying glass. When I inquired what the hell he was doing, he explained that he was doing a "Sherlock Holmes" on some grapes.

It seemed that Mr. Lorenzo had spent quite a bit of time looking at grapes through his magnifying glass. He contended that the grapes all had legs, and that they thought it was great fun to hide behind the tanks while the particular persons employed at my famous Napa Valley winery (and whom Mr. Lorenzo was ostensibly observing) cleaned the floors.

Then, when everything was clean, the grapes would run out into the open and roll around on the floor, laughing hysterically at the consternation they caused my crew.

I figured Mr. Lorenzo was nuts. After all, he had been drinking tequila steadily since the first day I hired him, and I never saw him sleeping, or eating for that matter. I judiciously decided that this was not the proper time to challenge some flipped-out psycho with a gun.

However, I was at the end of my rope two days later when Mr. Lorenzo, who had still not acquired any hard evidence on the particular people and their illicit liaisons, came up to me with a small hand-carved wooden flute of some sort. While I complained about the lack of results brought by his investigation, Mr. Lorenzo excitedly ranted on about his new discovery.

He claimed that this wooden flute he had fashioned could simulate speech patterns of grapes, and cause them to run towards the source of the sound. This, he felt, would enable my crews to clean them up once and for all, saving hundreds of man hours in clean up time.

Well, that did it. Here I was, the owner of a famous Napa Valley winery, listening to the rantings of some maniacal private eye, who was trying to tell me that he was going to save time for the very particular people that I was paying damn good money to expose in illicit liaisons with members of my immediate family.

Not only did this basket case tell me that grapes have legs, but he decided he was some kind of goddamn Pied Piper. When I explained all of this to him, he simply said, "Look, I'll call the grapes over, and you'll see for yourself."

With that, he tooted on his whistle, and I'll be damned if grapes didn't come rolling from all over the winery. Grapes were coming from under tanks and hoses, from must lines and from old drains. Within seconds, Mr. Lorenzo had a huge pile of grapes at his feet, and a big grin on his face.

I grabbed his whistle, and before he could stop me, I blew a few quick notes. Unfortunately, I had not noticed the five ton gondola of grapes directly behind me. We were immediately crushed by thousands of pounds of prime Napa Valley cabernet sauvignon grapes from my famous Napa Valley vineyard.

Somehow, Mr. Lorenzo extricated me from the pile, in spite of his own serious injuries. We now share this hospital room.

Mr. Lorenzo wants me to assure you that as soon as he recovers from his injuries, he will once again write his own columns. In the meantime, I hope this proves adequate.

Anonymously yours,

famous Napa Valley winery owner /s/

PART V

The
Interviews

INTRODUCTION

Back in 1977, when I first moved into Sonoma, I discovered a wonderful book, called *Great California Winemakers*. The book consisted of a series of interviews with famous winemakers. The interesting thing about the book was that every person interviewed was asked the same 30 questions.

As I learned more and more about the wine business, I decided to write my own book of interviews. I would ask my subjects different questions, but the focus of each interview would be the same.

I wanted to ask questions like, "When you come home from work, and sit down with your spouse and say 'I'm never going back to that job as long as I live.' What frustrated you to that level? And when you get up the next morning, and return to the job, what brings you back?"

I planned on interviewing grape growers, winemakers, cork salesmen, label designers, wine sales people, restaurateurs and wine shop owners. I wanted to cover the entire wine spectrum from farming to winemaking to sales. I figured that there would be a common denominator-- something that attracted people to wine, and something that made them successful at their trade.

I had a meeting with Larry Linderman, who does interviews for *Playboy Magazine*. He gave me a lot of helpful hints. Molly Sessions turned me on to Studs Turkel, which gave me a format.

I began the interviews, but then reality set in. Each interview cost $100-$200 to transcribe. I did five interviews, and transcribed four of them, before I ran out of money. Perhaps, someday a patron will give me the money to continue.

In the meantime, what follows are the four interviews. I don't know that they reveal a common denominator. I do know that they introduced me to a fascinating world of dedication and desire.

BRAD WEBB

An odd thing happens in the wine business. True
innovators pop up and have tremendous influence over
the entire industry, but rarely do they receive public
recognition. All too often the public attention goes to self-
promoters who merely copy the ideas of others.

Brad Webb probably did more practical work to
make fine wine in California a reality than anyone else in
the industry. As winemaker at Hanzell, he was the first to
use French oak barrels and stainless steel. He literally
invented inert gas technology, and he pioneered basic
development of malo-lactic bacteria. All these
winemaking components have become standard practice
in the industry.

Brad is a quiet man, but strongly opinionated.
While talking with him, I was constantly awed by his
brilliance. I found him to be very direct, and while he was
careful to credit other people along the way, I got the
impression that he was somewhat embittered about not
getting the recognition he truly deserves.

Brad Webb is the antithesis of my romantic notion
of a winemaker. He is scientific when I think of
winemakers as magical. But as scientific as his approach
to winemaking is, Brad remains totally impassioned. He
loves wine and winemaking. The industry is lucky to
have Brad Webb. It would not have become what it is
without him.

BRAD WEBB:
THE INTERVIEW

I was born in 1922, so I was in college when World War II came along. I spent most of World War II in school, first at Atlantic City for basic training, then Penn State College for more academic training. There weren't a lot of casualties among fighter pilots, so there was a surplus of fighter pilots.

They decided to turn us into B-29 co-pilots. That turnaround in my training took another year. I was on my last leave as a B-29 co-pilot when the first pilot got ill. We waited for him, although we were anxious to go overseas. Then VJ day came in the meantime, and left us all holding the bag with all this training and no war to fight.

That tilted my sense of indebtedness to the country, so that I stayed in the reserve. I got out of the Air Force, but stayed as active a reservist as I could all my life. That's been my only fraternity, you might say, the Air Force Reserve.

Meantime, I came back to California, and finished up my education in biochemistry. Tried to go to graduate school and found that I wasn't qualified, tried Berkeley and Madison, which was the top biochem school in those days. My grades were the problem. Before World War II, in biochem, I took a D. I was preoccupied with what was happening, getting drafted, things like that. I thought, "Well, biochemistry can't be really important." So I got a blotch on my record that stayed with me as far as graduate school was concerned. It was probably justified anyway. That set me off in the direction of practical research, rather than academic research. I probably would have found a spot for myself in the school system, otherwise.

Anyway, after graduating from Cal in 1947, I was offered a job with Professor Castor, Department of Viticulture and Enology at Davis. He was the bacteriologist. He filled the position that Kunkee now fills. He needed a technician for a year or two, so I signed on with him.

My brother was just getting his Ph.D. at that time in chemistry, and at the end of the year, he was offered a position in the Department of Enology. There was a rule against close relatives working in the same department, so I resigned.

It was a good one year job, but what I didn't realize at the time was *that* was the experience that led my career toward wine chemistry. A lot of young people don't realize that. Every step they take is in one direction or another. Hopefully, anyway, you don't go around in circles.

So, I left there and went to work for Julius Fessler, predecessor of Scott Labs, and worked the 1948 vintage. I remember things by vintages. In 1947 I graduated from Cal Berkeley, and '48 was Berkeley Yeast Lab working like an automatic analyzer. I was running two VA stills, an SO_2 still, two or three ebuilliameters, all at the same time. I remember having it worked out so that I could get about two drags off a cigarette between the time I'd light it and the time it would go out. Otherwise, I was dumping the ebuilliameter or something like that.

That's when I invented, but never... well, some of that got on paper. I worked out in principle the ideas of auto-analyzers, which I'm sure must have been, uh, all the chemists in the world were working the way I worked. They must have been thinking, "This is work for a machine, not a man." Since then, the Technicon Company and a lot of other companies, have produced autoanalyzers. You see more of them in the clinical labs than any place else. They're the logical outgrowth of that sort of work.

I should go back to point out that the B-29 was an automated aircraft, before the word was invented or used widely. It had analog computers, rather than digital ones, but it had a central fire system that was computer controlled, and a navigational system that was computer operated.

The B-29 was built that way. Kind of a wonderful experience to be acquainted with, to get used to the idea of doing mechanical things that way. So, I approached the job of winemaker too mechanically, many times. Too much from a point of automation, trying to see if I could apply automation, and I'm still doing that. I enjoy it, but it gives me a definite point of view, maybe different from other people.

Anyway, the vintage job tapered at Berkeley Yeast Labs, and I was offered a position at Pommerelle Company in Seattle. So, the first time, practically the first time, I walked into a winery, I was in charge of production. What that really did was reveal to me my ignorance. I had to ask the cellarman what we were going to do that day, and what we were going to do tomorrow.

You see, these people from Seattle had come down to get a California winemaker. I was hired as a winemaker/chemist on the basis of my experience in the lab at Davis and in the lab at Berkeley.

Things were very different in those days. The average number of enology students was four or five in all, and a lot of those were foreign students, surprisingly. The status of winemaker was about the same as pizza chef. I don't mean to demean pizza chefs, but winemaking was just an ordinary job, nothing glorified the way it has been since. Maybe that was wrong. It seems we're going in the other direction right now.

Anyway, I certainly didn't know all the things there were to know about making wine, although I'd helped my brother make some at home. I had studied the subject, and was familiar with the lab work, and had experience with a wide range of samples that came into Davis. That was good experience, but it didn't tell me what to do each day, and didn't give me the necessary personality to become a foreman, and I pretty well flunked out of that job.

I left Seattle after two vintages, but I really was going back to California to learn how to make wine. With my Seattle experience with berry wine, and having learned many of the problems, and the mistakes a person can make, I went to a great place to learn how to do basic winemaking, and that was Gallo. That's where my education in winemaking started.

I was in charge of the fruit and berry wine production. Later on, I took over the vermouth production from Bill Bonetti. I was there from '51-54. That transition was very traumatic, coming back to California, with the knowledge of how much I had to learn.

At Gallo, like a lot of other people in the wine business, I learned the basics of winemaking. What they'd really done is apply the scientific method in making the best possible wine, using the grapes that were available, at the volumes of scale that they're interested in. There's a tremendous story to be written about the Gallo's technique, someday.

What they've done is about as revolutionary as Henry Ford's application of mass production. You might say it's mass quality control in the wine business, on a scale that compares with the French production of *vin ordinaire* bulk wine in their co-ops. And in quality control, Gallo is ten times better than the average French co-op, not that I want to insult the French.

It was a pleasure, and a very demanding experience, working there in Modesto. A little like Marine boot camp in spirit. In other words, everything was very demanding, and finally I realized it took more energy than I had to continue to put out, and I found myself collapsing about every six months.

At Gallo, you pushed yourself. Nobody really pushed you. When you saw Ernest and Julio both spending the time they did on the job, tasting and making sure everything was the best possible, you darn well put out on your own initiative.

I remember I had to have a man fired once. He was a Hungarian, I think, of the Hungarian nobility, pushed out by the communists. He was looking for an executive-type job. Because his family had a winery, he'd been hired. We got down to the place where he had to shovel some pomace. I picked up the shovel to show him how to do it, and he refused to shovel. It was a matter of principle. His circle didn't work with their hands. So, I had to walk him over to the office and have him dismissed.

For the most part, people worked themselves. The Gallos were setting the example. They worked hard as hell. The Gallos and Charlie Crawford, who's almost the same. They set a very high standard of excellence, and they backed it up with their money.

For instance, they had some white vermouths break down with copper instability for no apparent reason. I pointed out the volume of production in vermouth was low enough so they couldn't get away with using brass valves anymore. They needed to go to stainless steel valves. They spent several thousand dollars, just like that, on my recommendation. A lot of money in those days.

164

They understood, I'm sure, that quality involves a matter of taste, and it's necessary in large, mass production lines to have a uniform product. One of the things that got us into trouble when attempting to move upward in quality was that variations in the flavor were difficult to avoid if you wanted to make a wine that would be judged better than a top notch Bordeaux. Part of the quality of fine Bordeaux is the variation. You're talking about two different markets. One of them is millions of gallons, and the other is thousands of bottles.

We were always interested in knowing if the same quality control techniques would work in high-quality wineries, and I got a chance to try that at Hanzell.

I left Gallo, and spent the year with Walter Richert & Sons, Inc. It was the vintage of '55, learning how to do it in a very small winery. Rick knew everybody in the quality wine business. When they had a barrel or two that was a little different than the others, they'd sell it to us. We made some vermouth, and did all sorts of things trying to expand the business to the size where it would support two families.

I married Alice about the time I left Gallo, and we put our combined savings into this venture, and went just about broke. In fact, I was working nights for the Department of Agriculture as a strawberry inspector when Mr. Zellerbach decided to build Hanzell. When he had it well under construction, he decided he needed a winemaker, and I got that job.

I remember the interview pretty well, going over and over the point that what I wanted to do was make wine using the scientific method. I wasn't interested in racking by the light of a full moon, although people were making good wines that way, but I was interested in the scientific approach, and I knew there'd be some objections.

Finally, Zellerbach said, "Mr. Webb, I've gotten your point very clearly. I employ many chemists in my paper business. I know exactly how they work, and that's the way I want to go about making wine."

So, we had an agreement, based on my lack of knowledge in the fine wine business, practically complete ignorance, but with his ability to taste and discriminate what he wanted. I was going to make samples, and he was going to taste them, and then decide which way to go.

Our goal was to produce a wine that would rank with the best wines in the world. He was willing to back that in any reasonable way. He said, "Well, I won't air condition the vineyard, but other than that, I'm willing to do almost anything."

This was kind of flying in the face of reality. A lot of people considered the site too warm for pinot noir, and too warm, probably, for chardonnay, and still do. But I didn't know, and I thought it was a tremendous opportunity to justify the application of the experimental method of solving problems in winemaking. I felt as if I had been nominated by the Lord, perhaps, to represent all the biochemists and chemists and technicians in the industry to show what they could do in the way of producing a better product.

We sort of take that for granted, now. A lot of people understand the contribution of science to winemaking. So, now it's fairly conventional to expect scientific winemaking to go on, but at the time, it really wasn't. Even though Pasteur worked on wine, as well as medicine, the progress in winemaking hadn't nearly approached the progress or the speed in which science had progressed in medicine. I'm happy about that change, you know.

Q: Was there anything else happening in California that paralleled Hanzell's effort to equal the French?

There were other people going at it slightly different before us at Stoney Hill and Mayacamas. At Buena Vista, Frank Bartholomew was more interested in balancing the books every year than anything else. There was Martin Ray, but we were the only ones with the scientific method and the bucks to back it up.

We built a laboratory that compared in size to our fermenting room. We had a bigger lab than Sebastiani Winery. Some people didn't have any laboratories at all in the smaller wineries. They didn't even run SO_2s, So it was the first full, gung-ho technical approach to winemaking at a quality level that I know of. That went on for six or seven years, until I guess I made my reputation there, although I wasn't aware of it at the time.

When Ambassador Zellerbach died, I thought the whole thing had been a failure. I was quite pessimistic about what had been accomplished.

The Ambassador's number one goal was to produce an outstanding pinot noir, and I hadn't felt that the pinot noir was good enough to put on the market at the time. I had some other things I wanted to do, but that bulk wine went to Joe Heitz and he put it on the market with some things he called improvements, and the wine sold very well.

By 1958, the chardonnay was an unqualified success, but it turned out to taste very much like the very best French chardonnay. In fact, while Zellerbach was still in Italy, we were sending the chardonnay to the embassy in Paris. They tasted it there, and everyone wanted to know what part of France it came from. So, we knew we had something, and that made the Ambassador very happy.

He was willing to wait for the pinot noir to get around to the point where I thought it should get. I

167

wanted to see the fruitiness that develops in the bottle bouquet, in the pinot noir. Still takes about seven years to get that on average. I wanted to telescope that schedule.

First of all, Andre Tchelistcheff, Harold Berg and myself had done planning on the fact that pinot noir would throw sediment. We thought people wouldn't accept that in a California wine. I was pretty naive. I also figured the California consumer wouldn't put wine down to age. So, we had to go far beyond the French performance. We had to bottle age the wine too.

This is why we developed the nitrogen technology. We had glass-lined stainless steel tanks and an anaerobic sterile method of getting the wine into the bottle without the usual exposure to oxygen. The reason for this was to prevent the sedimentation of the pinot noir. We hoped to cause the bottle bouquet to develop in the glass lined tank, and then to transfer the wine into the bottle without any aeration whatever, not compromising the sterility of it. We didn't know how many years we'd have to age the wine in the glass lined tank, but I found out since it would have had to be about seven.

We were going to make the wine that way in order to avoid having the American consumer decant the wine. We thought we couldn't expect him to decant it, knowing it was from California. Fortunately, American wine consumers at the Hanzell level are much smarter and more considerate than we imagined.

Also, at the time, nobody in the industry knew or would reveal how to propagate the malo-lactic fermentation. We'd get the culture out of a good wine, but lose it after about two generations. There just wasn't a good culture medium. When you inoculated directly into a sterile wine, the bugs wouldn't grow, or if they grew, they wouldn't cause the malo-lactic fermentation to go.

168

No one could tell me how to cause a malo-lactic fermentation. I tried for two years to do it at Hanzell in the lab, and then I found out that the reason was that I was inoculating the wine, not the grape juice. I did this work in the lab. I don't think I took it up to barrel size until I actually had the breakthrough in January 1959.

I took this sample of grape juice that I'd inoculated with yeast and bacteria, and I ran a chromatogram on it. The malic acid was gone. I realized that was the trick. We had to inoculate before the sugar was all gone. I was very excited about that, and thought I'd won my Nobel prize.

I got ready to apply for it, but when I went to Davis, Professor Ingraham showed me a copy of a paper in some obscure French journal by Dr. Peynaud, who had done the same thing the year before. I'd just overlooked that French paper.

At that time, most others in the industry were maintaining that malo-lactic fermentation was a spoilage problem for California wineries. Mrak, Vaughn and Amerine all were very negative about it. They refused to recommend varieties of specific organisms. They were afraid of getting into a position that someone in the central valley would consider to be a recommendation for malo-lactic fermentation. They were correct, of course, from the central valley winemakers' perspective. Most valley wines needed more acid, not less.

I was working with what bacteria I could isolate from French wines, which wasn't very much, and I didn't identify any of them. Matter of fact, I didn't have that much experience in bacteriology.

The problem was my cultures wouldn't last very long. Progress started when Professor John Ingraham took on a project that finally developed ML34.

I remember holding a ladder in Louis Martini's winery while John and Louis went up to the top of the tank for samples, the very samples out of which George Cook cultured ML34.

Louis had a very reliable malo-lactic fermentation every year. I don't know if he fed back lees, or reinoculated, but Fessler taught me that it was very poor practice to feed back things like that. Certain breweries operate on the same basis. You can get a general infection that can put you out of business if you feed back continuously. What you're doing is contaminating the whole plant.

Anyway, the idea of a pure culture inoculation was an attractive one. Ingraham made the collection of about 30-40 organisms from wineries of good reputations. Martini and Wente are the only two that I know of for sure, but I'm sure most of the quality wineries were represented.

My uncovering the way to inoculate was only part of the victory. The other vital thing was Ingraham's discovering the Rugosa culture medium, which made it possible to culture all those organisms. I don't know whether he or George Cook was more responsible. Cook was Ingraham's technician.

Anyway, they developed this collection. I made trial fermentations using red wine on the entire collection, and George ran white wines on the whole collection. Something like 9 out of 10 red wines fermented. Only about 50 percent of the white wines fermented. We know now that's typical, but Ingraham and Cook were rather frustrated by the experiment. We put the whole thing together and published in 1960. Ingraham made me the senior author, which was very nice of him, but he did most of the writing.

I don't know whether that's the most important thing I've done in the wine business or not, but it was a turning point for me. After years of trying to do something, and always failing, you get a little discouraged. Then to have it pay off... it's like winning the California lottery.

I should mention Hod Berg, because Hod insisted that it was essential that we have malo-lactic fermentation, because 90% of the good French wines had it. Something like 30-40% of the white burgundies had it too. We found no correlation between malo-lactic fermentation and quality in the whites, but in the reds there was. So we decided not to do it in the chardonnay, but we'd do it in the pinot noir.

The '56, '57, and '58 Hanzell pinots did not undergo m/l fermentations spontaneously, which was interesting. Up to that time, a lot of people insisted that m/l bacteria came in on the grapes. Other people insisted that the bacteria were in the winery. By building a new winery, we could prove that if it didn't go, the winery was the source of the fermentation. So, in a sense, we proved that. Of course, the reverse has been proven too. I think everybody now understands that it can happen either way.

The other thing that was important at Hanzell was understanding about barrels. I've been trying to teach this to winemakers ever since I started work at Hanzell. The mechanics of a barrel are fairly complicated, and very important to winemaking.

The first thing a lot of people don't understand is exact volume of a barrel depends on the outside air temperature and the radiation heat exchange going on. Heat can travel by convection, conduction and radiation. So, for a barrel sitting in the cellar, minor changes in air temperature don't make much difference, but changes in radiation intensity do.

The reason is that the barrel is a system of elastic wood compressed against steel hoops, and the precise diameter of the hoop depends upon the precise temperature of the hoops, and that can change quite rapidly. When I started measuring barrel volumes, I found that the volume of the barrel was going up or down depending on whether the lights were on or off in the room.

I had to rebuild the air conditioner at Hanzell, because it would cycle about every two minutes, and every time it cycled, it made a 5ml volume difference in the barrel. As soon as there was some ullage in the barrel, air could leak in. Gases can go through crevices that liquids can't. So, the cycling of that air conditioner would pull some oxygen into the barrel. The oxidation rate was higher because of a cycling air conditioner.

My concern at the time was with aging and oxidizing the chardonnay while it was in the barrel. One of the first things I found out was that there was no humidity control. I had been outsmarted by the engineers and the architects in the construction of the winery. I had asked for a vapor seal in the wall, but they left it out for fear the wood around it would mildew and rot. Nine out of ten times when I specify vapor seals in buildings, it's been left out by the actual construction crew.

Anyway, I had to fix that. I tried to get 90 percent humidity. I'm basing this on, "When in doubt, when there's absolutely no information, go to what they've done in France."

By the way, we weren't the only ones that had French barrels. Martin Ray had some. He used them, and I know there were a few at Beaulieu and at Krug. So, everybody knew about French barrels, but Zellerbach was the person who generally gets credit for introducing them, and *all* of his wine was aged in French barrels.

Robert Mondavi and Joe Heitz keep pointing out the importance of French barrels, but to me the most significant thing that happened in those days was the development of the nitrogen technology. That was kind of the outgrowth of my experience with Gallo, and people have credited me with inventing the nitrogen use in the winery. I'd be happy to take credit, but I know that a fella named Morrie Turboski, who was the winemaker at the old Madrone Winery, had nitrogen cylinders, because I saw them when I was delivering some material for Berkeley Yeast Labs.

The nitrogen technology we developed at Hanzell was a little different from the way anti-oxidation technology developed in Napa Valley. Their approach was centered around sparging with nitrogen to take oxygen out after it's been picked up through leaky fittings and so on. The Hanzell approach was to prevent the access of oxygen in the first place.

Q: What is your feeling about intentionally oxidizing wine?

Well, there are times when that's desirable in red wine production, many times. There are probably some times when that's desirable with white wine production, but not very often with chardonnay.

I think oxidation is part of winemaking, but it should be controlled. I just can't understand why you should not operate knowing what you're doing, especially when you can quantitate something so easily. I think if you're not doing anything else, you should be measuring something. It's silly when you *can* control some variable, not to control it.

I believe in running SO_2s on red wines. Some people didn't, a lot of people still don't, but it's a winemaking variable that is important for the winemaker to know. Anyway, your control of oxygen is an important thing that started at Hanzell.

Stainless steel fermenters pretty much started there, depending on whether you consider Hanzell commercial scale. Those were the first I know of. Pete Peters of Valley Foundry put a lot of effort into the design of the winery, and hasn't gotten enough credit for it.

You know, a lot of people weren't ready for stainless steel in those days. When Zellerbach's friends would come into the fermentation room, and see a row of stainless steel fermenters, they'd say, "Dave, what did you do? You've got a hospital here."

Q: Describe the Hanzell method of making pinot noir and chardonnay.

Well, the unique thing about the pinot noir was the controlled malo-lactic fermentation. Still is, I guess. And the unique thing about chardonnay production was the skin contact. Some people like to call it maceration.

As soon as they got the chardonnay crushed, we'd start taking samples of the juice, run into the laboratory and run a tannin on it. We'd start plotting a graph and watch the tannin come up, sampling every 15 minutes or half hour.

When it got to a certain level, I'd press. Since the free run is so limited from those tanks, something like 60-90 gallons per ton, all of the press wine went back immediately into the free run. I simply didn't have the time to press it as long as they did in Europe, and with the stems in there stirring the press cake was impossible. So we pressed for 15 to 30 minutes, then drove the rest of it out. It would still be dripping wet.

Q: Were the stems used strictly as a press aid?

Yeah, with the understanding that it may make a slight difference in the taste of the primary pressing. The press at Hanzell is a basket type press, which means quite a traveling distance for the juice to get through the pomace, so it gets lots of filtration.

I think the Wilmes press is a breakthrough as far as quality is concerned. It gets more potential out of the grapes than the Hanzell-type press. I would never go back. It was a pity that the junior size Wilmes press wasn't available at the time we built Hanzell. We really tried to get one, but they wouldn't make one for us.

Q: What did you do upon leaving Hanzell?
I was offered a job as a tour guide at a Napa Valley Winery, and a job in Albany doing research concerning grapes, but it seemed like too much of a commute. So, I took a job as a research assistant over at Sonoma State hospital. I sort of gave up the wine business and went back to biochemistry. Inside of a year, I was making more money than I'd ever made in the wine business. I thought I was set up for life, and I was real happy.

Zellerbach knew that Hanzell was so small that he was never going to make enough to support me the way he wanted me to be paid, and the way I wanted to be paid. So, he said, "What you've got to do is make a good reputation, and become a consultant." So I was a consultant from day one at Hanzell. I worked with Lee Stewart and for other people too.

When I left Hanzell, I got a letterhead that said, R.B. Webb, Biochemistry-Enology, and started a consulting business on weekends. So, I was working at the State Hospital, enjoying having the proper tools for a biochemist for the first time, but the wine business started getting hotter and hotter, and my weekends became fuller and fuller.

Finally in '68, Chuck Carpy at Freemark Abbey made me an offer that I couldn't refuse. I asked my boss at the State Hospital to match it. He couldn't, so I went back to the wine business.

175

Freemark Abbey let me go back to school, to re-educate myself as far as technology was concerned. I'd gotten out of date in biochemistry. Most of it happened since I got out of college. Freemark Abbey gave me a full time wage for half-time work. For the next three years, I spent half my time going to Sonoma State, and half consulting with Hanzell and Freemark Abbey. Most of the time at Freemark.

Q: What's your favorite part of the winemaking process?

I guess getting it into the bottle when I know it's being done right is the most satisfying, because it's been the most difficult. It's the most underrated by the general public. Getting a good cork, and getting the bottle of wine filled in optimum conditions is not easy to do. It's almost completely ignored by the public.

Q: Did the wine business intrude in your family life?

Well, yeah... it's really difficult to put into words, but there was a time when I was really feeling guilty, because yeast works 168 hours a week, and I was only working 40-60 hours a week. I thought the least a winemaker could do would be to work as hard as the yeast.

At the same time I was getting complaints from the housekeeper that I wasn't showing up for meals on time, and my kids were strangers. I was feeling the same thing myself, that life is going on, passing by very rapidly, and I wasn't spending time doing things that everybody likes to do in a family way.

That was a definite complication that I tried to resolve in favor of the family. I'm not sure they know that, but I limited my participation in things and spent more time at home.

I had a serious operation. Came out of surgery with all sorts of tubes connected to me, vibrating machines, a pretty traumatic experience. Recuperating from that, like a lot of people, I straightened out some goals in my life. I tried to simplify my life, and decide what I wanted to do. At that point, I started spending more time with the family.

Q: What were your goals in the wine business?

Generally, to apply the scientific method to winemaking. To make a living. To make better wine. To introduce better wine to more people.

For a winemaker, I have kind of an Okie background. I grew up in Victorville, CA., and I was down there last year to an old timer's meeting. Nine out of ten people at the dinner table really didn't understand what quality wine was all about.

I had to explain that good table wine helps make the family stay together, because it makes eating dinner more fun. It's almost as simple as that.

Q: What do you drink at home?

I like a glass of sherry before dinner. We use that as an appetizer. Occasionally, if I've got a very good excuse, I'll mix a martini that's half vermouth and half gin. Otherwise, we drink wine.

We drink about 50% white wine and 50% red wine, but about 80% of the white wine is chardonnay. In the reds, more cabernet, zinfandel and pinot noir.

Q: What age range do you like to drink?

I like a bottle of four year old chardonnay. About six or seven year old cabernet. Zinfandel depends on who makes it and what the particular vintage is. I'm kinda interested in zinfandel of almost any age. There's such a wide range. It responds to the soil so differently. It would depend on where it was grown and how it was made, whether it was to be aged or not.

I used to have a petite sirah from Freemark Abbey, still have some. A lot of people try to hold that for ten years to age out the tannin. I still like it best when it's fairly young, even though it has a huge tannin in it. You almost have to wade through it. I like the flavor better when it's young.

Q: What winemakers or wineries do you respect?

I'd like to put it the other way around. I don't know anybody that I disrespect. I think that's universal. It's one of the remarkable things about this business. Since I've been in it, I've only come across one guy who wasn't proud of what he was doing.

One of the things you've got to be careful about when talking to winemakers is everybody does the very best he can, and he regards his product almost as highly as he does his children. He's proud of what he's done. He's done the best he can with what he's got. You can't fault a man for doing that.

Besides, we make wine to our own taste. You can't argue with taste. Quite often, maybe he's drunk enough of it, so he's overlooking or simply forgets the minor flaws in his product.

So, I've only met one fellow who was ashamed of his product. His employer made him work in a certain way that led to the wine being poorer than it needed to be. He later went on to make some great wines.

Q: Did you question your ability to create great wine year after year?

No, I don't think so. I'm not very good at tasting. I'd go to work some mornings and taste, and until I got the sample I *knew* was good to standardize my palate, I thought suddenly the wine had turned to vinegar or something.

Q: Where does the romance in the wine business come from?

I don't know. From a biological point of view, I have to suspect it comes from the fact that there's ethanol in wine. Partly, that makes wine mysterious. Alcoholic beverages have been historically related to religion.

Wine has a lot of other things going for it. One of them is the cornucopia, mother earth, mother bountiful image that wine evokes.

The other point is the relationship between wine and food preservation in general. One of the things wine did for primitive cultures was to make available some fruity flavoring material that is healthy in the winter time, particularly in the centuries before man was able to preserve fruits, even by drying. Wine in the winter time would represent the best approach to the fruit that he had in the summer time. It must have been pretty attractive from that standpoint.

At the same time, wine is medically healthy and beneficial. It purifies water by dropping the pH. It kills pathogens and prevents bacteria that spoils food from contaminating your gut.

Q: What do you dislike the most about the wine business?

The worst part of the wine business, to me, is a certain amount of deceit and confusion--attempts by some people to take advantage of the quality image, and project themselves a little higher on the hog than they are.

The thing I like best about the wine business is knowing I can help, that my services are valuable. I'm proud of the fact that I've never asked anybody for a raise in pay. I've just showed up for the job and done the best that I could.

I realize I have a lot of personality limitations. Like I said, in Seattle, I never got over the threshold of becoming a foreman. I just never felt comfortable being that politic a person.

I didn't think it was necessary to perjure myself that much. The foreman, like a politician, has to do a lot of fence straddling. He has to keep a lot of people happy, doesn't have time to expound the full truth of the matter to everybody, so he has to oversimplify, to falsify in a strict ethical sense. It's beneficial to everybody, causes people to get along, but it's one of the things that makes me uncomfortable, my inability to socialize. When I get some minor success that way, I feel much better about it.

Q: What do you think of awards and medals?

I'm amazed that they are as effective a merchandising tool as they are.

There are some assumptions in judgings that are implicit. One is that there is such a thing as quality, any one wine that everyone would regard as the best. This may not be true.

Enter 100 wines with 100 judges, and conceivably each wine could appeal to one particular judge, and he would regard that as a super wine worthy of a gold medal. There's no necessary reason why everybody should regard one wine as being the best.

Q: What barometer do you use as a measure of your own success?

I guess it comes down to the attention and respect I get from other people in the industry. Though, to a certain extent, you've got to be happy with your own estimate of your own success, and to hell with the rest of them.

I swear it was in Churchill's obituary in *Life* magazine, but somebody asked Churchill how he ever went to sleep during World War II when so many lives were riding on his decisions. He said, "Well, you get in bed, have another brandy and another cigar. Finally, you just turn over and say, 'To hell with the sons of bitches.'"

BOB SESSIONS

Bob Sessions is Jake Lorenzo's idea of a great winemaker. Bob works at Hanzell Winery atop a spectacular hill overlooking Sonoma Valley. History aside, Hanzell is breathtakingly beautiful. Bob Sessions could have been a pompous, self-centered ego-maniac selling his few precious bottles of fine wine for exorbitant prices.

Instead, Bob is as down to earth as a person can be. Sometimes, he is so self-deprecating, that I feel like shooting him. I couldn't stand the loss.

Bob strives to make the finest wine in California. On occasion, he may have done it. He is driven in his quest for excellence. He is steadfast in his beliefs about fine winemaking. He does not hide from high alcohol. He seeks intensity. He chooses to make his statement and then stand behind it.

Bob Sessions is essential to the wine business. His love and respect for the craft, along with his simple, down-to-earth dedication should serve as the shining model of behavior to up and coming young winemakers.

Outside of Sonoma, people are unaware of how we locals revere Bob and Molly Sessions. No reader of this book could make a better vote with his or her dollars than to invest in a bottle of Hanzell wine and give thanks to Bob and Molly Sessions.

BOB SESSIONS:
THE INTERVIEW

The romance of wine comes from the drinking of
the wine. I think it's the axis of going from ground to
pleasant taste to good feelings. It's all pleasure. The earth
is the earth, and that's something you can't even describe.
The pleasure part, the good taste, and the feeling that the
alcohol gives you. As much as people knock alcohol these
days, take the alcohol out of wine or beer or any beverage,
and you've got nothing. It's funny that kind of nice
feeling that you get. It's tied into the transformation of the
grape into alcohol, into this thing that gives you a good
feeling.

My entrance into the wine business goes back to an
old friend, a high school buddy. We stayed in touch after
we got out of high school. I graduated in '49. Dick Van
Bolt and I stayed in touch through the next several years.
Dick was going to school in Switzerland, and after I
graduated from Berkeley, he asked me to join him for a
few months travel in Europe.

When we came back, we both got jobs around San
Francisco, and then he got this job at Mayacamas. He had
planned to go down the coast and just be a bum for
awhile, but he went up there to work for the Taylors in
'59. He stayed there for 5 years.

Molly and I got married that same year, and it
became a second home to us. We visited up there a lot on
weekends. I went through five or six jobs trying to find
the *one job*. You know, as an English major, you either

183

teach, write, or do nothing. Nothing seemed to be my choice.

I was a cook, an ambulance attendant, a clerk, and a whole lot of other things. I was a bank teller, and I was a Department of Employment interviewer.

So, that's what I was doing in '64. I got into that job from the bank job, because... I'm not sure I am anymore, but I was idealistic, and I wanted to make the world better. Those were the Kennedy years, and although I could see some of his flaws, his call to try and help touched the people in those days, and I was one of them.

So, the best I could think of, my limited abilities and everything, the circumstances where I was, was to go to work. I think I'd been counseled once by somebody in employment as part of collecting unemployment, which I used to like to do in between my several jobs. This was in North Beach, and I was kind of impressed by this lady, so I thought, "Well, jeez, I wouldn't mind helping people out like that." Not that I got so directly helped, but I liked her approach.

So, I thought I'd go to work with the Department of Employment, and try to help. Well, shit, for awhile I got that feeling, but then the bureaucracy of it just began to burn. Then, just looking at years of this, I couldn't see how I was going to make it. I was just going to have to leave.

Then this thing with Mayacamas. We'd been going up there every month for five years. I'd been working in sales up there, and on the bottling line, and harvesting during my time off. Dick decided to do the opposite, go to the city from the country, because life finally got too dull for him, I think. He went to New York, and he and his friends and my wife talked me into taking his job.

The job was to manage Mayacamas. Dick had been co-manager with Bob Ellsworth, but Bob left, so Dick was sole manager. He was working up there with Kim Giles, who was the vineyard man. Bob was the winemaker, but he left and there was no winemaker for '64. Dick hired Brad Webb, and Dick and Kim made the wine in '64 with Brad consulting.

In the meantime, they were talking to me about going up there. I told them, "I don't know how to do any of these things." I was pretty good at figures from my bank work, so I could do that. Well, anyway, they talked me into it. Mayacamas was supposed to hire a winemaker, and I would be the manager. Kim and I and this winemaker, this third unknown party, were going to do the work up there.

Dick just sort of dumped me on the Taylors and said, "I'm leaving. Here's Sessions." They knew me enough to trust me, but I think they were leery about every other thing, as far as my abilities and this whole winemaking bit. But they were stuck. They were living in New York. They'd been living there for a couple of years trying to make enough money to keep pumping into Mayacamas.

I went out there, and the guy they'd hired to be the winemaker was some mountain guy who liked to talk and drink and philosophize more than he liked to do any work. He didn't work out at all. He was a neat guy, but he just didn't work out. He had been the cellarman, but he hadn't learned anything by the time I got there.

Kim and I decided we'd make the wines. Brad was on the scene by this time, and he consulted with us. Together, we made the '65 wine.

After that, Kim went off on a trip around the world. He never got past San Diego, but that was the intent. So, that left me, and by that time I decided I was a winemaker, 'cause for two years I was just losing myself in the Mayacamas job, and loving it, and reading and everything, going through whatever I could, pulling it off.

The important thing was how much I liked it, how much I loved Mayacamas. Being up there, being on top of the world, literally. That part of the world, anyway, and that whole mountain experience--10 miles out of Napa, half-hour drive to anywhere, and then eventually being the only person up there who could do anything. Looking back on it, I can see how I got caught up in it, and became totally dedicated to working in that place. I worked every holiday, unless we were having parties. It wasn't just work; it was part of my life.

And I learned. I became a winemaker, and instead of hiring a winemaker, I hired a guy to do the office work, and shipping and things like that. So, I was making the wine, living my life up on the mountain.

Bob Travers bought the place in '69. I worked for him for three years, but it turned out to be too small a mountain for two guys who wanted to do things their own way.

So, I split and went to work for Souverain in Rutherford as production manager. I worked there for the '72 crush when the winery was just being built. That was my one year of big winery stuff. I'll never forget it. Especially when you've got just one hose for water, and you're using a generator for electricity, and you're crushing 750-800 tons. At Mayacamas I was crushing 50-60 tons. This was a completely different experience.

You're putting up wooden tank uprights the day before you use them. It was an experience. I didn't like it as enjoyment, but it was a good experience. I left though, because after the harvest I decided I really didn't like this. I didn't have a lot of respect for some of the goals of the winery, to get big fast. Just make it fast, and sell the wine as fast as possible.

After that, I went to work for Warren Winiarski for a while helping him with the construction of his new winery. Then in 1973, Brad Webb came and told me about the Hanzell job.

Brad had been Zellerbach's winemaker at Hanzell since 1963. When Zellerbach died, Brad started his consulting business. Dick hired Brad as a consultant at Mayacamas, and that's where we met.

Here at Hanzell, he was well established as a frequent consultant. I think his pattern was to come in once a week, more if we needed him. We worked well together. I always liked Brad, and he was easy to work with. He sometimes was too smart for me, but he was too smart for a lot of people. I mean he would get going on these technical ideas, and I could hardly follow.

But Brad was fine to work with. He really had a nice way of not making you feel like an idiot when he could have sometimes. He'd let you know if you didn't do something right, but he was easy to work with that way. You'd be scared to death of what you'd done, thinking this guy's going to find it out and everything, but he made my mistakes less painful than they probably should have been.

He had tremendous self-confidence. That's why I had confidence in him. So, I didn't really question his judgment very much. A couple of times I might have done things differently, but as long as we worked together, I don't think it happened very often.

Brad left when the new owner Barbara De Brye bought Hanzell. There was a certain amount of hard feelings involved. It was a shock to me. I was pretty nervous about it at first. I thought I could make the wine all right, but I really had this sense of the Hanzell image. Brad was very image conscious, and he passed it on to me. I worried about what Brad's leaving would do to the Hanzell image.

Once I got over that, then it was a question of just whether I could make the wine. That wasn't a big problem. It really wasn't.

First of all, I'd learned Brad's "Hanzell ways" very thoroughly. I'd been through two crushes with him, so it wasn't that hard. I had all the background on top of that. Primarily, it was the competence of decision, my decisions. When you have a Brad Webb consulting, and you think it's time to bottle, and he says you're right, then I think it's time to bottle, no problem. Or something like that. A thousand decisions to make, so that was the hardest thing.

I took care of that partly by using Kim Giles as a consultant. Mainly, I wanted someone to taste with, and Kim's a good taster. Kim had made wine at Hanzell for five years, so I couldn't think of anybody better, and we've been friends since Mayacamas days. Old friend, five year winemaker, worked with Brad, so it was Kim. He still comes up, and we have a tasting panel. So, that took care of things.

Q: What makes Hanzell wines special?

Like everyone else, I think the vineyards are the big deal. I think it's the small number of grapes we have on the vines that make for the good wines we have up here. I know there are exceptions, you can get more tons per acre and make good wine. We get about one and a half to two tons per acre. I really think it comes down to that.

Fourteen acres of vines are 30 years old. We have some acreage about 12 or 13 years old, and then a new vineyard around 10 years old. Average age is about 20.

We have good clones. I'm a big believer in clonal differences in wine, and I think a lot of our deep color and flavor is clonal, not just the way we make the wine or where it's grown, or even the way it's cropped.

Probably, it would be hard to overcrop these vines. We don't over fertilize minerally. We don't irrigate, and I think that's a big part of it. We'd have to make agreeable wines no matter what we did. The question is, "Are they going to be great wines?"

To me, that's the whole excitement in the wine business, whether you can make a great wine. I really don't have a lot to say about winemaking. I could sit and babble, but if I say it right, it's simple.

We're automatically going to make a good wine up here. The excitement comes from trying to make a great wine. There are other goals, more housekeeping goals, like making sure you don't fall on your face, and making sure Hanzell keeps going the way they expect to, but I think the excitement comes from--hell the whole purpose of it is to make a great wine.

I'd hate to be working for a winery that had no pretensions of making a great wine, a place that doesn't grow great grapes and doesn't go out and buy them. After the initial charge of excitement you get when you start as a winemaker, making the great wines is the only thing that makes it worthwhile.

Q: What is the Hanzell style, and how do you get it?
I'd use the same words as the book, the style is full-bodied, high varietal character, rich, with a long finish. At least that's the attempt. If those four descriptions could be fulfilled every time, that would do it for Hanzell.

I know I left out balance, and I should put it in, but sometimes balance is used to mean a wine that doesn't have much else. Balance seems to take care of itself.

What we seem to do up here, and I say seem, because sometimes these things happen in spite of what winemakers might want, is go for a lot of varietal flavor. There are people out there who think this could take care of itself. They complain about the wines being too hot or too alcoholic, but I think without that much sugar, we wouldn't get as much of the full body and fruity varietal character that I like in our wines.

In pinot noir, there's the Hanzell way, and then there's the experiments. Actually, I guess the Hanzell pinot noirs are the Hanzell *and* the experiments. I don't know when I'm going to stop calling them experiments. Anyway, the Hanzell way is to pick at 23.5°-24.° Brix, ferment at 76° to 80° F until the skins have lost their color, that's usually about five days. We punch down four times a day, at least. Then we press. The sugars are hovering between five and ten. The pressing is medium. It's not real light, but it's hard enough that there's not much juice left. We don't separate free run and press juice. I separated it one year, but I was not at all happy with that one experience, so I'm not going to do it anymore.

Anyway, we press between five and ten sugar going into a tank, and we inoculate with malo-lactic starter. We keep the wine around 70° F artificially with warm water, and then rack as we need to according to the lees. We always rack, because we've had problems coming out of our ears if we didn't, so by the time malo-lactic is finished, we've racked two or three times. I taste the bottoms of tanks continuously for possible sulfides. We usually get done in four to ten weeks. After a post malo-lactic racking, the wine sits around for a little clarifying until I have empty barrels for it.

That's the Hanzell way. That's how Brad Webb passed it on. We've made some great wines that way.

We pick the chardonnay at about the same sugars. We give them eight to ten hours in the holding tanks with the skins and stems. Then we press that night. The juice settles for two to four days, decision based on timing. Then we inoculate with Montrachet yeast and ferment at 52° to 55° F.

Then we wait. Some years fermentation is faster than others. 1985 was extraordinarily slow. It was a bad year, the worst since '80 for getting the chardonnay dry.

Anyway, we ferment in stainless steel, and then after fermentation has stopped entirely, or my analysis shows there's hardly any yeast in them, we rack them, fine with bentonite, and go on to barrels.

The first couple of years with cabernet, I made them just like the pinot noir. I didn't stop and think of how I'd made cabernet at Mayacamas, and I just punched the shit out of the cabs. We had two tannic monsters come out. Neither one we felt we could release. They were the '79 and the '80.

So now, the temperatures are perhaps a touch cooler than pinot noir, around 75°, and I'm experimenting with them. Frankly, I don't feel competent yet at the "Hanzell way" of making cabernet. The '81 was made pretty much like the pinot noir with less punching down. It wasn't much different, and it was fine wine.

As far as drinking our wines, I think four to eight years is a good drinking time for Hanzell chardonnays. Obviously, they can go longer, but I think it's a good sound drinking time.

Pinot noir has two drinking times to me. It's something between four to six years where they seem pretty drinkable. Then they go into a funk. I'm not sure exactly where they are, but I would say between eight and fifteen years, they taste really good again.

Q: Do you ever question your ability to pull off a vintage, year after year?

Constantly, all the time. If you want a one word answer, yes. That's one of the negatives about this job. I mean, I have confidence, yet I question my ability. It's funny, 'cause I know it doesn't take too much to slip.

Hanzell has such a reputation that I can't make any mistakes. The pressure is there. It never ceases or levels off. It just seems to increase all the time. We're all caught up in the game of winning. I mean, I'm talking in terms of making the best wine there is, but yes, I question it.

Sometimes, I wish I owned a winery myself. One thing about being the proprietor is that if you make a mistake, your pocket book takes a beating perhaps, and your ego may take a beating, but there's not going to be anybody else telling you, "You made a mistake under *our* name."

Now, that's never happened here at Hanzell, but it will happen if I make a mistake. People are really supportive, they really are, but I live with that.

I am definitely a hard critic on other people's wines, and it's a cliche, but I am my own worst critic.

I will argue the benefits of our wine, and I get pissed off sometimes, because people get so caught up in certain styles of wine that they forget what's good about ours.

I think one of my best attributes as a winemaker is a really high demand for quality. I think I can recognize quality. I can't always analyze it that well, but I can recognize it, and I recognize it in our own wines. I'm real hard on it as it goes through the process here.

Sometimes, I wish I had more ability to go from head to verbal in describing wine. There's a certain analytical ability that I think I'm lacking. Maybe it comes from just inherent limitations, and maybe it comes from not having an organic chemistry background, and therefore a certain lack of confidence in myself about this. I'm always looking over my shoulder at myself, about whether I know enough about wines, after all these years, to be making these decisions. It's awful. You think, jeez, anybody can come up and do this.

Another attribute is just detail. You have to have the mundaneness of mind to hang in there on a lot of boring details, those things that if you don't do it right now, then it shows up in the wine way down the line.

That's where I can't believe some people. Well, first of all, they haven't learned that they've got to do that "now," right now. Then, when they have not done that "now," and it messes up their wine, they release the wine anyway. They let the world see how dumb they can be.

I would swallow that wine. Maybe I wouldn't if it was my money, but I would certainly advise our directors to swallow it. I'm already thinking of a wine I might advise them to swallow now, but I'm in my worrying mode.

It's why I mentioned sometimes wanting to own a winery. As an owner you can *not* release a wine. You can sell it in bulk and not get as much money for it, but you don't have to release it. You can also go ahead and experiment, and have a blockbuster of a wine. Or you could pull back for awhile. That's kind of fun.

I don't have that freedom here. That's the drawback of the job, but I can only remedy it by owning the winery, and I'm not about to own a winery. But I can't do that here, at least I don't feel I can.

That's why I was talking about the experiments. I do have experiments, and they have come to affect the style. Maybe the wine has changed to some degree, but I still can't. For example, I couldn't come out tomorrow with a barrel fermented Hanzell chardonnay. I don't feel I could, not without talking it over with the owner.

Q: What exactly does being the winemaker at Hanzell entail?

Well, first of all it's making the wine. I do everything with the wine--no, I don't, now. I don't top the wine anymore, but I was topping wine up until about three years ago. When we started coming in with the new vineyard's grapes, I began to use somebody more and more for those things, and actually when I'm racking now, I'm farming that out a lot. I'm taking tests there and everything, but I'm not actually doing everything.

I used to do everything. If I could lift the barrels, it was just a question of loading them up, and I'd do that too. There's been a transition period to a point now where I don't.

But I certainly consider myself the winemaker in every other sense. I'm not just somebody who comes through and says SO_2 for that, tastes, and does the sampling. But the physical work, I guess I'm passing that on.

All the decisions are mine. I use Kim, my assistant, and Molly as soundboards, but the final ones, the ones you sit back and go home and say, "OK, what do I want to do?", those are mine.

Molly does things for me, but I also do the posting. I do book work. She does a certain level, and I take it over from there. She does a certain level of marketing, but I do the final crunch stuff.

I make the decisions that determine if people are going to buy a wine or not buy a wine, and so forth. It may look like it takes care of itself, but there's a lot of work in selling wine here, too.

In the vineyards, I have Nicolas and Jose, but again the final, less so perhaps than the winery, all the final decisions are mine. I try to encourage a lot of freedom of decision out there. Although sometimes I get out there and say, "No, do it my way. I don't care what you want to do." But physically, I'm not out there doing much. I still may, disc or sulfur, because of employee breakdown, but primarily I'm out of that. I did a lot of that stuff at Mayacamas, and a lot more here at Hanzell over the years.

The other stuff... I have to make sure the toilet is working down at the house. I may have to get the kitchen stove going, because the owners are coming up.

Those are silly examples, but there's a lot of stuff that goes on, a lot of visitors, and I have to make sure that everything is OK. I'm in charge of the gardeners.

Again, Gary does gardening and I don't, but still, in the final sense, I have to decide how much money to spend and what has to be done at certain times. I wear the "estate hat" a lot around here.

There's no question, winemaking gives me the most pleasure. The best thing about crush is that I have this unchangeable reason, this unalterable reason for not answering any phone calls, for not being consultable by anyone or anything. Molly knows that she can't come up and ask me any questions, or certain types of questions when I'm working. The door is shut to everybody else, and all I can do is work, make wine. It sounds sort of goofy, but that's really the most fun.

First of all, it's the focusing. I get to focus myself on one thing. Even if that one thing was something else, I'd enjoy it more than having myself get--I mean, around here, this little bucolic winery, you'd think, "I'll just go around and convene with the stars," or something like that, but I feel sometimes I haven't any chance to focus. I go this direction, that direction.

It's partly because of my other life, too. Sometimes, life on the planning commission gets in the way of winemaking, which it shouldn't, but it does. Being on Bundschu's land use committee, you know how those things go. And I've got to get my tennis in, too. My kids get on my mind, and that kind of thing. But I love it when I can just close the doors at work and say, "I'm winemaking, don't bother me."

I have a sign I put up that says, "Don't disturb!" in three languages. It's primarily during crush, but sometimes because I've had it with phone calls and everything else. I hate the phone. So, I just put that sign up, and nobody's supposed to come through here. They do, but they're not supposed to. So, I like winemaking the best.

I think I could like this grape growing. It could be a contender. I don't think it would win, but I don't do the actual grape growing so much. At Mayacamas I did a lot more out in the field, and I learned the pruning and everything. I really liked that kind of thing. I like being on the tractor. I did do it at one time. I like it all. I like the variety of this job. I love the fact that it's based on farming, but I probably like more that it isn't 100% farming.

Q: What's it like working in a business with your wife?

It's tough. We're better now, 'cause we're both getting older possibly, but it's tough. It's rewarding at times. We come home, both put our feet up, and talk about what a hard day we had, and we know what the other is talking about. But sometimes, we get so involved in our own worlds, we both think the other one doesn't appreciate what our world is like.

The hardest thing is that I'm her boss, and I might have to say, "Look, I'm not your husband talking to you now, I'm your boss, dammit." And she'll react as if I'm her husband. She'll deal with me on a personal level. It's the same way I'd say it to Jose or Gary. So that's the hardest thing.

But this business blurs the line between work and your personal life, My personal life is primarily my kids. I have other personal life, other interests. I don't mean to sound like a one-dimensional person. What I mean to say is without kids, it would be like Mayacamas. It would be so intertwined that one wouldn't be able to be separated from the other one. 'Course, up there, we were living there, so friends would come up. I'd work. I'd play. It'd be the same thing.

That's why I mention the kids, because Molly and I get enough time together. I get enough time for my own pursuits, my physical pursuits, but I really appreciate being at this job and in this business, so I figure you've got to take some negative stuff with it.

My one biggest resentment that I'm beginning to see, is the short summer, because of these early harvests. I never complained about it before, but especially when it looked like we were gonna have another short summer this year, I figured another year with six weeks out of a twelve-week summer. It's hard to find time to do all the summer things here, and get away with my family. And it's mainly family that bugs me, because my kids are going to be going away someday, and I want to enjoy them as much as possible. But for them, I wouldn't have any resentment for this job.

In fact, the way I am right now, I really do feel it gives my life a lot of form and meaning, this job does, my work does. I think if I didn't have it, I mean if I couldn't work here, but had enough income, I'm sure I could become a beach bum, too. But as it is, it does, it gives me a lot of order. I like order. I like disorder, but I only like it when I can leave it and go back to work.

Q: Do you drink wine at home?

All the time. We try other people's wines as much as we can. Molly and I are pretty much in the habit of our pre-dinner drink being white, although we slowly are changing over to red.

Molly, more than I, prefers white to red for dinner. She's also a little more conventional. She likes to have red with red meat, and white with white meat. I am definitely evolving towards pinot noir with everything.

But I do love chardonnay. I love it. I like some sauvignon blancs, and other wines. I like all varieties, but I figure there's only so much I can drink.

When I go to somebody's house, I'll drink anything, but since there are only so many good chardonnays and cabernets, I tend to stay with those wines.

Q: Which winemakers and whose wines do you like?

I've always had great respect for Dick Arrowood. If there's any problems there, I think it would be the clones of chardonnay.

I like Mike Grgich. I respect Michael a lot, because of his pride. I think Mike turns out good wine, works hard at the wine, and that's important.

I know an old guy I won't mention in Napa, who is well known as a winemaker, but he's never been obsessed enough. He's always had the brains, but I don't think he loved wine, really loved wine. You've got to love wine. There are a lot of people in the business who don't love wine. They drink it. They like it, but they don't love it. That's a big difference. You might turn out some good vintages once in awhile, because you can't help it, but you've got to love the wine.

But the wines, Grgich is one. I like the Bundschu merlots and cabernets. I do, very much. Caymus, great wines. I put them up there with Arrowood, not for the same reason, exactly. Bill Sorenson at Burgess Cellars turns out a great white wine. He's a quiet guy, and he has to do certain things, because he's just a winemaker, but he does a pretty good job.

Oh, hell, the conglomerate at Mondavi. You have to respect them. They've been managing to get it done.

I like Chalone a lot. They used to have an inconsistency that put me off, you couldn't count on it, but I think they're finally on track, say '78-84. I put them right out there.

Carneros Creek was at one time my favorite pinot noir. I don't think they are quite up there as well as they used to be either. I can't quite figure out why, maybe they're getting too involved with other things.

Q: What do you think about fairs and awards?

We don't enter fairs. First of all, when I got into the business, fairs didn't have a very good name. There were all kinds of charges about people making small lots just for fairs and so on and so forth. So, I didn't go into this job with a good feeling about fairs.

Since then, fairs have come around, and they're quite above board. But in the meantime, when it comes to fairs I think we have nothing to gain, only something to lose.

I get pressure sometimes from the directors. They want me to enter. They think that other wineries can't be as good as we are. We have to be the greatest, so if we could bring home a gold medal, that would perhaps satisfy them.

But my argument so far is that if we enter a fair and we get a gold medal, people will say, "Well, what did you expect?" Some people will say that. But if we don't win a gold medal, aha! A silver or a bronze, you've got nothing. I think panels are just human, and from day to day we can change our minds on wine. Same thing's going to happen with a panel. Several people, day to day experiences, they might not like our wines that day.

So, I think judgings prove very little. They just give people medals to sell wine with. They keep an interest in the wine business, but I don't think they prove much.

I rely on my own palate. I'm very prejudiced with my own palate. I've tasted a lot of other chardonnays and pinot noirs and now cabernets just to see where we are, and I think that in California we're right up there in all those varieties. Sometimes I like our wine almost best of any. Other times I like it in the top ten or the top six. I don't feel we ever fall out of that group. I know I've seen tastings where judges say we fell out of it, but I don't feel we did.

Then I get so much feedback from people. We're constantly being told how wonderful we and our wines are by letter and telephone and by going to tastings and things like that. I like to go to tastings 'cause I love that feature. Even though people will tell you your wine is the best at a tasting, and even though another group will tell another winery theirs is the best, you don't hear those other people, so you go with it. Also, I go down and I taste and I know we make damn good wine, and I feel good about. I really do.

What I like best is when people say that they've been drinking our wine for years, and they always think it's one of the best. I like it when they say it's the best wine they've tasted this year, or something like that.

To me, a compliment, probably the highest compliment I could receive, would be something that would compare my winemaking up here with the past Hanzell. You know, someone says the wines tasted good for 20 years, or they taste better and better. Or they say, "I always liked Hanzell." I like that. It means I have the feel.

MARCELO HERNANDEZ

Marcelo has been a friend of mine for 15 years. We shared a philosophy to work hard and become the best at what we did, for no other reason than the simple pleasure it gave us to do the job the way it should be done.

Marcelo is a strong, quiet man. He is the hardest working man I have ever met. I have seen him on his back, in the mud of a field, working on a broken tractor with numb fingers. I have seen him working in a zombie-like state, because he had not slept for 3 days. I have seen him deal with a crew of 30 diverse individuals, without ever once demeaning them or showing them a lack of respect.

Marcelo tells his own story, with a single-minded, quiet pride. Going over the piece reminds me that Marcelo Hernandez paid me the greatest compliment of my life when he said, "Lorenzo, you work like a Mexican."

After working in the grape business for all these years, Marcelo harvested the first crop of merlot from his own vineyard this year. The smile of pride on his handsome weathered face is something I will never forget.

MARCELO HERNANDEZ:
THE INTERVIEW

I first came to Sonoma in 1966. I came up from
Tijuana to visit my brother. He was in Fairfield, but there
was no work there, so my brother and I came to Sonoma
for the first time.

Our first job was for Jim Bundschu. We picked
plums for a week or two, I guess. Then after Jim finished,
I worked for Mr. Charlie Spumer.

At first, I was just picking grapes. Later after
harvest was done, I started driving tractors for Mr.
Charlie. He taught me how to drive all kinds of tractors
and Caterpillars. When pruning time came, he taught me
how to prune. So I drove tractors for him all the time, and
then Mr. Charlie Spumer made me foreman.

See, Mr. Charlie had lots of small places. He rented
the places, or leased them. Mr. Charlie would plant the
grapes, and grow them, and sell them. Then, after a
certain number of years, the people would own the land
again.

So I was the foreman. I did the disking, spraying,
pruning, everything. Mr. Charlie taught me planting,
then how you grow grapes, and how to prune. See, he
pruned different. Most of the places didn't have any frost
protection, so he taught me to leave three buttons on each
spur.

Most of the grapes were head pruned in those days.
We worked at all these different ranches. One of the
ranches was Jim Bundschu's. That's where I started
disking. Mr. Charlie had lots of small places. Some of

203

them he rented or made a contract or something like that. He planted, and kept it for 5 or 6 years. This is the way that Mr. Charlie Spumer worked, and this is how I learned about the grapes.

I worked for Mr. Charlie about four years, I guess. My wife and kids lived in Tijuana. I visited them every month, month and a half. Depends, you know. My wife couldn't work there, so I sent money every week.

After four years, I moved back to L.A., because Mr. Charlie got sick and stopped for a while. I didn't have any work, so this is why I went to Los Angeles. I went there for 13 months. I worked in a factory where they made French fries. Well, not French fries, frozen potatoes for fries in the drive in.

After 13 months, I called Jim Bundschu one day, and I asked him for a job. He knew me from when I worked for Mr. Charlie, so he said. "Yes."

I came up here to Sonoma in August, and I talked to Jim. I explained that I came back to Sonoma to try to find somebody to help me. I really needed help with a house, because I couldn't find a house with eight kids. So, since he knew me for four years, and he sees how I work, he decided to give me the house and the job too.

When I started up here with Mr. Charlie Spumer, I only had a passport. The passport wasn't good for working, only visiting. So the work was illegal, see. Later Mr. Spumer helped me with resident papers. He gave me a letter, and I went to the consulate. I had everything, all my papers in order. The letter was good, you know.

Later, Jim helped me the same way for my kids. He gave me another letter, and I went back to Tijuana in 1972 with the letter. I took it to the American Consulate in Tijuana, and they gave me the papers for all my kids. We moved up to Sonoma and lived in the house on Jim's ranch.

When I came to work here, Jesus was the mayordomo, but I can't work with this guy. It's difficult, you know. With some people it's real difficult to work together. Their ideas aren't right. Everybody has their own idea about how to do things, but his way and mine were always different.

This Jesus quit in 1981. I don't know why he quit, but it was just after Jim's father died in '81. I was working in the winery with Lance Cutler when Jesus quit. Jim asked me to take Jesus' place.

I didn't want the job. It's too much responsibility, but I know most of the workers, and I know the grapes. So, I took the job of mayordomo.

Well, Jim gave me this responsibility, because he knows I have this experience with grapes. You know, growing grapes, pruning grapes, and taking care of grapes. I know a lot, because Mr. Charlie taught me.

Like I said, he pruned different because he didn't have any frost protection. This is why he left three buds on each spur. The idea is when the first shoot comes in, the others aren't ready yet. So, if the frost comes in, and the shoot is already up, you lose the first shoot, but there's still the other two. They're not up yet. I think this is good.

I worked for Mr. Charlie for four years, and every year we did the same thing. The last year I worked for him, it frosted a lot, but we still had some grapes. The first two buds were all done, but the last one came later. We had some grapes. Not a lot, but some. He didn't lose everything. That's why we pruned that way.

When I became mayordomo, the first thing Jim showed me was the pruning. He taught me how he liked it, how he wanted it. But he prunes different, see. It's simple, real simple.

I still like the way Mr. Charlie taught me, but Jim tells me how he wants to do it. He has his idea, so I don't use my idea, because if I make a mistake, it's his grapes. So, all the time, I let Jim do things however he wants.

One day, Jim said, "Let's sulfur tomorrow."

I told him, "Jim, I think it's gonna be too hot tomorrow."

He says, "It'll be OK, let's sulfur."

So I do it, and the next day it's real hot, and the vines burned. This happened two or three times. Sometimes, I work together with Jim, and we figure how to do something, and it's OK, no problem. But sometimes he does what he wants, and we have problems. It's not my fault, 'cause it's his orders. He told me to do it, and it's his grapes.

I make mistakes too. When it's my idea, and I do it the way I want, then it's my responsibility.

Q: How do you hire the workers?

Most of the time, I hire the people, the pruners and the pickers. Lots of times, somebody gets a job, and they're fairly good. They come up to you and say they've got a cousin or someone who wants to come up. Like Salvador, he's from my home town in Mexico. He knows I'm here. He knows my brother. So he goes to my brother and gets my phone number. He'll call me from L.A. or Tijuana asking for work. When I have something for them to do, I hire them. My cousins came up. My brother. Some other friends. Everybody wants to stay here, see.

One problem is people will work for us for two to three years. They go back to Mexico for one or two years.

Then they come back here and expect the same job, see. So, the guys working here will get mad if I do it.

One guy, I found him in the road, laying down under a tree in the shade. I say, "What are you doing?"

He says, "I'm looking for a job. Do you know anybody?"

I say, "Yes. How did you get here?"

He says, "Well, I come from Mexico. I don't have a car, but I came from Mexico, and I need work."

Well, the next day we started picking, so I hired this guy. He worked for us for two or three years. Then he went back to Mexico. The first time he was a good worker, but when he came back he wasn't so good.

Q: Is it hard to get workers, now that they're required to have legal papers?

In my opinion, it's the same. It's easy to get papers, whether they're real or not. Last harvest, I never had any problems. Lots of people are asking for work.

Q: How do they get paid?

When I first came here, everybody picked grapes in buckets. Two buckets made one box, and I think a box paid 45 cents.

Each picker had a card, and for each box the card would be punched. The problem was they would try to be smart, to cheat. The guy punching the ticket would punch extra for his friends, so they would get paid more. Jim lost too much money. He paid for too many grapes.

I saw this problem the first time I came here. There were lots of people cheating. This is why I told Jim Bundschu all the time when I saw this problem. I told him to do it different, but he never did. He figures that it's easier to pay for a few extra tons of grapes.

Finally, Jim tried to change the system, but I didn't think his new system would work either. Jim decided to pay by the pound. Everybody picked together, all the groups. Everyone worked together, and they divided the money.

The problem with this system was the smart guys wouldn't fill up their buckets. Every time they dumped their buckets, they weren't full. So the other people make the money for you, because everybody works together. This was a big problem, and everybody was mad.

This is why I changed. My idea was to pick in teams. Usually a team has eight guys. This way, there's no big problem, because the group is small. If somebody doesn't work as hard as the others, the pickers will say to take this guy away and get them someone else.

Everybody in the group gets the same money, but because the group is small the pickers can watch each other. So this is the best way because it's easy.

Now, when we pick, we use three groups. I have time to check on every group. If they leave too many grapes on the vine, I have plenty of time to tell them to pick better. With the three groups I have plenty of time.

Q: What's the hardest part of your job?

The hardest is harvest, 'cause there's too many moves, you know. We have four ranches. Sometimes I pick at Cabo, and then we have to move everybody; tractors, gondolas, pickers and everything.

It's hard to be organized, because you've got to check the groups while they're picking, but you've also got to plan how you want to start again for later, and for two   or three days. Just thinking like that is the hard part.

Pruning time is real hard, too. I have to work every day. Even when it's bad weather, everybody has to work every day. It's hard. It's not easy working with a group of people like that. It's real hard, 'cause somebody wants to work, somebody doesn't want to work. Somebody wants to work half day. Somebody wants to work all day. This is a problem.

They come to me all the time. I try to be nice and take it and organize things. I try to plan a job. I think about how to organize it, and how to finish it in a certain time.

See, sometimes Jim tells me to do a job. He tells me to get somebody to do it. I gotta think about how. A job for one or two guys is easy, but a job for five or six guys is different. You've got to think about a job with five or six guys, cause if you don't organize five or six people, you lose a lot of money. One hour or one extra man, and you lose too much money.

You've got to think about how to put these people to work. I mean right away. If people stand around and time passes, it's no good because you lose a lot of money. So I like to put one guy at this ranch, and one or two at another. But five or six guys together is more of a problem. Somebody's always walking around, and they lose time and they just don't care.

I can't work like 20 years ago. My energy is not the same. When I start to do something, I want it done. Whatever I do, I want it done. This is my thinking, see. I don't have the same energy, but I do it any way. I just do it. Some day, later, I won't be able to work any more, probably. I don't know. You never know.

Now I don't work so hard. Not like before. But I want to do something, see. So this year I have an idea.

Last year at pruning time I put somebody to spray Benelate. This year I do it myself, 'cause this way I walk every row. I follow everybody, and I know who is pruning right and who is pruning bad. So if a guy is pruning wrong, I know it and I can tell him, "You don't do it right."

Because I spray every vine, I see everybody. I see how these guys do it, whether they do a good job or not. Some guys, not too many, but some guys never try to learn.

But the hard part is when we pay by contract, piece work. Everybody's got to be followed all the time, 'cause when they try to work real fast they do a bad job, see.

Last year, Jim paid by the hour. Everybody worked by the hour. But those guys weren't happy, 'cause they didn't make money. You can't live on $5 an hour. That's one person and everybody has a family, but that's all Jim would pay.

By contract everybody makes more money. A little bit, not much. But it's harder for me, 'cause I've got to watch all the time. If I have something to do and I go away for an hour maybe, when I come back a bad guy can mess up. When I'm there everybody does it right. This is my idea. I spray this way so I can see. I try to do the best.

Q: Do the guys like working here?
Yeah, I think so. If somebody found a better job, where they could make more money, they'd leave. Other places I know pay more money, especially for pruning. Now, I think Jim pays all right. Everybody makes $70-75 a day or $65-70, it depends.

Q: Does this job take you away from your family?
Not really, 'cause the kids are busy too, all the time. So I don't think they miss me. Everybody works, see, nobody stays home. Some kids are in school, and the others are working.

Q: What do you think of raising your kids in America?

It's a hard question, a real hard question. Not for me, you know, for my kids. I don't have nothing in Mexico, nothing to leave. I don't have land or anything, so I left to work.

For my kids, I think there is good opportunity. Lots better here than in Mexico. Problems are the same. People are all the same, no matter what. There are bad people in Mexico and bad people here. There are good people here and good people in Mexico. Everywhere it's the same. The difference here is that it's more free.

I came here to work hard and make money, but I can't make money 'cause I have too many mouths to feed. I make enough to live, but not to save.

Those kids have better opportunity than I, 'cause they speak the language. It's the important thing, the best, see.

In Mexico, everyday it's hard to live. Everyday cost more and more and more. This is why Mexico's economy is real hard. You can't make enough money to live there.

Like my brother. He made good money, but he can't live. It's too expensive. He made more money than a lot of people. He made more than the minimum. He worked all the time building houses in Mexico. So, he made the contracts and he made the money, but he couldn't live 'cause it was so expensive because of inflation.

Inflation goes everyday, you know, so he's got to make more money every day, so it's impossible. That's why he came here. He tries to stay here.

Q: Did your kids face a lot of prejudice growing up?

No, I don't think so. Some, like Carlos and Ricardo just starting off, and then it quit. Not bad.

Those things happen in the big cities like Los Angeles, San Francisco, Chicago. This is a small town. Everybody knows everybody. Santa Rosa is bigger. It has more problems than Sonoma, but not my kids. Some of them, yes, a long time ago, when we first came here. 2 or 3 guys, you know, but not for a long time. Those things don't happen here.

Q: Do the workers face prejudice?

I don't know. Sometimes people think Mexicans are bad people or something like that.

A long time ago some police stopped me in town with a friend, and he asked me for my papers. I asked him, "Are you police or immigration officer?"

He got real, real mad. He says, "How about your friend?"

I tell him, "I don't know." I think he's legal.

The policeman says, "Does he speak English?"

"No."

"Ask him for his papers."

I talk to this guy, and he has nothing. No papers. So the police take him out of my car and put him into the police car. I say, "Hey, it's not your job."

He stopped me for speeding, and he forgot to give me a ticket, but he took the other guy. I don't know why.

Q: What are you proud of when you look at your job?

A lot of people don't know nothing about the grapes, but I know everything about grapes. If I quit Jim's place and go looking for a job, nobody needs to teach me how. That is my pride. I know everything about the grapes. I don't say I know it better than everybody, 'cause maybe some people are better than me, but I know grapes.

Q: Do you like your job?

Well, there's a lot of problems. Working with people is real hard. I'd prefer to drive my tractor again, instead of running entire groups. It's real hard. I don't enjoy being the boss.

But at my age, if I quit and try to get another job, I'd have to make the same money. I don't think I could make the same money if I went to another place running grapes. So I need to stay to make as much money. So it's not a problem, but I think about it.

Q: If you didn't have to work for money, what would you do?

If I had a million dollars, I think I'd go around the world, to know the world, and probably help somebody who needs money. Real poor people. Things like that. And work in my garden. That's it.

CHARLES HOUSE

Chuck House is simply the best label designer in the business. He is also the most fun to work with. We first met in a record shop where Chuck was painting a logo he had designed on a wall. His greatest contribution may have nothing to do with design or wine labels. It could well be that introducing Jake Lorenzo to African music will somehow out live Chuck's artistic accomplishments. However, I doubt that will be the case.

Any lover of wine is familiar with Chuck's work. Frog's Leap, Viader, Clos Pegase, Etude, Laurel Glen, Whitehall Lane, Antinori, Plam Vineyards, Creighton Hall, Morgan, Gundlach Bundschu Reserve series, Bearitage and all of the Bonny Doon stuff are creations of Chuck House.

Chuck's job is to take how owners and winemakers feel about their produce, and translate those feelings into colorful pictures. That he succeeds as often as he does is a tribute to his talent and dedication.

Chuck's vision is, how shall I say it...unique. In this interview, he explains everything. The trick is in the deciphering.

CHARLES HOUSE:
THE INTERVIEW

I was born in Newport, Rhode Island, at the U.S. Naval Hospital. I grew up in the Midwest and spent some time in West Africa. My dad was a teacher at the University of Nigeria during my teenage years. It was a great wasted opportunity, because I could have been investigating all this rich, local heritage and culture. Instead, I was just getting interested in girls and other typical teenage stuff.

In a way, the fact that I lost a lot of opportunities there made me more aware that you can lose opportunities, if you let them pass you by. I felt very badly that I didn't take more of a chance to really learn about local music and native art and culture.

I was so interested in my own feelings. I wanted to know what the Beatles were doing, things like that. But having had that great lost opportunity made me very aware of not losing any more. In a sense, it may have affected the way that I got into art and design.

I went to Justin Wall College, a residential college within Michigan State University. I graduated in anthropology, and I never had any art training, but I found that art was something I was interested in. Not in any classroom sense, just in terms of remembering things. I seem to be real interested in learning about art and trying to figure it out, remembering what Cezanne's stuff looked like and what Van Gogh's stuff looked like, and learning about the history of it.

215

I remember thinking to myself that you have to do what you like in life. It's not really a matter of what you're trained to do, or what you feel you should do. You have to go where your greatest interest lies.

I really liked packaging too. Little artifacts have always interested me. Little trinkets and packages. There's something humorous about them, and yet very profound in terms of providing a key to unlock something about people's lives. I found myself getting less interested in Art with a capital A, famous artists and classical techniques, than with disposable art; art that is a part of its time and a part of its culture and then goes out of fashion. It's almost as if that provides a greater key to the people and to the times than something that was designed to last for eternity. So, I found myself getting very interested in packaging.

In the meantime, I worked in Michigan for the Parks and Recreation Department. I was mowing lawns, and I guess my first commercial art was painting cartoon characters on playground equipment. That was a great job. I just loved it, and I loved the fact that it was on playground equipment too. That was a big part of it.

We moved here to California, and I just had very vague thoughts of going into some sort of commercial applied art. I went into business as a sign maker. I did a lot of sandblasted signs, and a lot of hand-painted signs for businesses. A lot of those are still around in Sonoma on the Plaza.

They're pretty good, really. I fabricated a lot of wood and tried to make them real three-dimensional, and use a lot of creativity in designing them. I enjoyed doing that, but I eventually felt that the printed piece was more what I was interested in, and what I was good at.

With the signs, I found that I could sort of put them together, but I wasn't really a skilled craftsman. I'd just

216

lay awake nights thinking that my signs were going to fall
and kill somebody or something, and it just didn't seem
worth it to me. I wasn't getting that much money for it,
and the constant worry of, "Are these signs gonna self
destruct?" or "For how long am I responsible for these
things?" was driving me crazy. Of course, the same
things happen with the printed pieces as I found out, but
at least it gets out there.

It's something I really wanted to do, to affect the
mainstream of graphic design. I wanted something that
would be seen in a lot of places, and to get out there to
more people than those that would pass through a single
spot. So, I wanted to get into books, magazines and
packaging design eventually. Although, at the time, my
expectations weren't high enough to consider getting into
something like wine labels.

At this time, I was working for my brother-in-law,
who owned Vintage Image publishing house. I was
packing books in the warehouse, just trying to be open to
an opportunity if it came along. There was a lady who
needed some rush work done for a catalog that was
coming out at Christmas, so they needed an extra person
in the layout department to do real simple layout and
paste-up. I sort of taught myself as I went along.

I had been taking classes at the JC. I took an exten-
sion program in printing to learn how to use the printing
press, just so I'd have an understanding. I was really just
trying to be ready when my opportunity came, to be able
to sort of step in, to work in that environment in an area
where I wanted to work.

Of course, no one likes free labor better than design
and publishing studios. There were occasions when they
were putting together a project, and it was a matter of
coming up with a lot of things to show somebody, so all
on my own, I would submit things for free on the possibil-

ity that they might be accepted in whatever eventually came of that. I did a lot of that.

I also designed a portfolio specifically for Colonna and Farrell Design Studio. They were associated with Vintage Image, and have since become one of the big names in label design. I spent hours meticulously crafting this little wine label replica. I did a couple of them. It would have been unbelievably expensive to do that under actual conditions, but knowing the kinds of things they needed, I was able to form a very specifically directed campaign at this one place to get them to hire me as a designer.

Of course, the terms were such that I was basically working on speculation, and getting paid only for what I sold, and not working for salary or benefits or anything like that. I was just willing to work real cheap to do something that I really like to do under the assumption that I would eventually start getting things into print. I would eventually start to have a backlog of material, things that I would have done that could build and lead to other things. My wife was working as a nurse, and I was working as a manager of the apartment complex we lived in, in addition to doing this design sort of part time. We were able to make ends meet and hang in there. Pretty soon, I started doing some pretty decent work and getting paid sort of regularly.

I liked being able to earn money by cutting up little bits of paper and putting paint on paper and fooling around with type. I've always been real interested in typography and the design of letter forms. To be able to juggle these little design elements in front of me on a desk is a very playful activity. Having worked at jobs where there was a fair amount of drudgery and looking at the clock waiting for the day to end put a unique perspective on being able to do something playful and earn money for it. I liked that aspect best.

I also like the idea that I could be affecting the course of design history, in a sense. I've always felt that my ultimate goal was to, in fact, influence the history of graphic design through my packaging.

Wine is something that gets out and is seen by people in decision-making positions, and to people influential in the worlds of art and science. It's reproduced in quality magazines, and it's something that really gets out there and into the flow of not just national, but world design. It's very influential.

I liked the idea that I could be sitting at my desk playing with little colors and bits of type and it eventually would be printed and then go out all over the world. Everybody who saw it would be influenced by it, and some would ask who did it and call up the winery and say, "Who does your design work?" So in that sense, I've always done my work on the basis of how I want it to reflect on me personally. That's what I like best about designing. I found it was a very nice way to spend your eight hours working.

I learned a lot at Colonna and Farrell, both for the good things that happened, and for the bad things that happened. I found that we would get the client's requirements in a very abbreviated form, and maddeningly so, because we were the ones doing the actual work of interpreting their concepts and trying to create ideas for wine labels.

We all did work on various levels on these projects, but it's very difficult to interpret a client's needs if you haven't spoken with the client. That really formed the cornerstone of my own philosophy when I started doing this for myself. It was a matter of getting out and seeing people and being able to read between the lines of what they expressed as far as their requirements went.

I found that frequently what they asked for wasn't what they really wanted, and there were subtle clues in the ways that they expressed their wishes that gave me hints as to what they really were after. Just by looking for clues in their environment and the way they dressed and who they were, and asking questions about seemingly unrelated matters, I could get at the heart of what was different about their project.

I found that there were a lot of things that are the same about every project, but in order to really create a personality for a wine package, it's a matter of finding out what's unique about the approach. It doesn't necessarily have to be a unique way of looking at the wine, it can be any seemingly unrelated clue in their history, or their past, their heritage, their taste in art and music. All these things can provide some little angle.

I like the problem-solving aspect of it. I had never been enough of an artist to have an inner need to express a personal vision of my own. I don't find art to be, for me, that kind of thing I need to express myself, nor do I find the need to express myself in words that much. I'm more of a consumer, I guess. I don't feel that I have a burning vision that the rest of the world needs to experience, but I do like very much interpreting other people's ideas and creating something for them that's beyond their dreams and expectations. My goal is to provide them with something that's a lot better than they envision.

In that sense, it's more of a problem-solving analytical function, and I really enjoy that. I always liked Sherlock Holmes, and the thought of him collecting these little cigarette ashes and things, and that being the key to the whole mystery, and going to the heart of the mystery is where you will find the solution.

Anyway, after a while, people started to talk to me directly. It became obvious that somebody other than the people they were talking to was doing the actual design work on a number of projects. People began to approach me directly. I met some people like Lance Cutler who were kind enough to introduce me to other people in the wine industry. The Frog's Leap project was something that Lance got for me directly. So it was a matter of meeting a few people, and once again, being ready when the opportunity presented itself.

Eventually, I just got too busy with my own projects to continue working for the Design Studio. There were no benefits, real poor wages, and it was just time to move on. I've been busy ever since.

I haven't even had time to do a business card, because I've been so busy working for everybody else. I've never done any self-promotional work at all, so that's one tribute to the word-of-mouth network, and to the philosophy of putting all your efforts into the best possible job. Good work will bring in more work. That's really the only way to do it.

I've always been suspicious of self-promotion, as I think everybody is. It's a necessary defense mechanism in our society to disbelieve everything that you hear people say about themselves. It's like in the rain forest, we had to learn to identify the sound of an approaching jungle beast. In America, where you grow up watching 14,000 hours of television before you enter grade school, you have to learn not to believe what people say about themselves. In a consumer society, you're heavily influenced by advertising, so I've never believed what anybody said about themselves. It's more a matter of proving it in the context of the work that's actually accomplished.

I was fortunate with the Frog's Leap label. It was the first real job that I had done completely from the beginning, with my own sense of art direction, and realizing that I knew best. It was the first time that I did something that wasn't anything like they told me. It was the first time I trusted my own design sense, and it was the first time that I realized I had reached a point where if I thought it was good enough, then it probably was good enough. Not that it was the best thing that ever was, but good enough.

At that point, I wasn't as busy as I am now, and I had a lot of time to think about it and work on it. I probably earned minimum wage for that project, if that, because I spent so many hours just thinking about it, going through reference materials, trying to find something that really struck an idea.

That label was very influential. A lot of people called me after that, not just in the United States, but some international clients as well. There have been other labels and projects that have gotten attention, but that definitely was the big one for me.

I don't really know exactly how to explain the nature of what I do. I know the feeling I have in my work is very much an up and down sort of cycle. There are times when I'm real excited about what I'm doing and real proud of what I've done, and there are other times when I feel I just don't have what it takes to really do the best job possible. I'll see other things people have done that just look a lot better than what I'm doing, and I'll have a real feeling like I just am not working at that level.

If I have a feeling that my work is not good, I have no option but to take that and increase the quality and the level of expectation in my own work. If it's that I don't have enough time to do it, that my projects are too rushed, I have to be serious and tell people that I just need more time to do it, or that I just can't accept the project. That's my hardest challenge. Because in every project, you never know what's going to be that great opportunity to do something wonderful. So I have a very hard time rejecting anything.

I've been on my own for more than nine years and I've never turned down a project. Right now a project I'm working on is for a gourmet dog food called Poochie Smoochies. I didn't reject that, so what can I say? It's crazy. It's like, maybe I can do this great little dog biscuit package and it's just going to be the cutest, funniest little thing that anybody ever saw, and I'd be an idiot if I turned down this project.

That's the backlash from not doing any self-promotion. Everything comes as a referral from a friend, or from a client, or from somebody who's a mutual acquaintance. Or they've seen work they like and just feel that you're letting down this entire chain of acquaintances and business relationships if you don't do it. I've really got to get serious about this one of these days, but the main thing is that the quality level has to be there.

There's almost nothing that I've done that I don't think could have been improved. I don't think there's a single thing I've done that, if I could, I wouldn't go back and adjust it in some way. Now, that's not to say that the adjustment would, in fact, be an improvement, because a lot of times I've had projects where I have had time to sit and look at them and analyze them and then make changes. Frequently, those changes are not for the better. Sometimes it helps to do them all quickly, and just let it all flow together. So, I don't think that time is necessarily an ally. In effect, you can get into a syndrome where you create a sense of self-doubt, so you make changes in your original concept, and it turns out that those changes are not for the better. It is true that in striving for perfection, there is never a moment when you feel you've really achieved it. I think that's part of what keeps you going.

You're always trying to come up with something that you're really happy with.

Often time is the critical factor. You just have to make the time. You work all day, and then you realize, "Hey, I've got all night!" It's like a luxury to realize if you really need it, you have those hours between 9 p.m. and 6 a.m. that you're not doing anything with. I mean you're just sleeping. There have been many, many times when I have used those hours to great effect. You just have to have the time to do it.

I often think about hiring someone to help me, but part of my problem is that no one can really do what I do. I'm convinced that there's nobody in the world who can actually interpret people's needs and translate them into wine labels anywhere near as effectively as I can. I've come to the conclusion that there's absolutely nobody who can really step in from my level down, even in the sense of handing something over for layout and paste-up. There's always the chance in dealing with the actual type that you can improve the quality of the project. I've found that some of my best improvements have come on the layout and paste-up board, just designing with the actual typography and illustration with the placement of it.

In fact, the way I work now, I start out designing with all the typography in place, and do the layouts from the beginning design phase right on the layout drafting board, so that's it's actually built up from the framework. It's like you're constructing a house. You don't put the decoration on first. You lay the foundation, and you build the framework, and then you see what the essential structure you're dealing with is. Then you can go and elaborate on it. So I find that everything from design down to production is something that I need to be hands-on involved with. So, I will always just do that by myself.

Q: Step by step, how would a project evolve?

I would start by conducting an interview with them, asking them a lot of questions. I have no forms for this, but just asking about their interests and what they hope to achieve for the winery and some kinds of mundane things about their target markets and things like that. Asking if they have any specific interests, trying to do some detective work in getting a handle on what they really want, and looking around their office or their house and seeing the kinds of things they have on the walls, the books they have in their bookshelves, clothing that they're wearing, a lot of things I'm actually learning independent of what they're telling me.

That's the first key. You have to have some solid insight into what they like before you can determine what's going to be the best solution. A lot of times, getting people excited about their own project is the big key to creating a successful marketing program. It has to look good to the consumer, but the people that get out there and sell it every day have to be excited about it too.

Once you have that concept, you can outline the specifics in terms of typography, what's actually going to go on the label itself. At that point, I would make some rough notes for about 20 ideas, and those would come partly from what I observed from the client. I would then take that list of my mental notes and match it against a similar set of mental notes I had about things that I've seen lately that I really like.

Texture is real important to me in my work, and I like the idea that you want to reach out and touch something. It's like ceramics, if you're in a shop that sells fine pottery and it looks great, you just want to pick it up. That's the idea behind wine packaging. It is a sculptural unit. At its best, you should just want to pick it up and hold it, and cherish it and enjoy it for its appearance alone.

There are a lot of keys to achieving that, and as I said, they come from ceramics. They come from fibers. They come from textiles and pottery, and there are great marble textures on tombstones, and great carpeting. You'll be walking through a home and you'll see some real interesting Persian rug or something. These things I have a similar mental checklist in my own mind. I go through a match-up requirements of great things that I've seen that I think would make a dynamite label, match it up with the things that they've said, the type of approach they want.

My feeling is that everybody should have a chance to reject a very conservative approach, and to also reject a very adventurous approach if they so desire. But everyone should have those two options in any given presentation. So that when they pick what they want, they will feel that they're choosing from the outside limits. That way they feel good. They don't feel, "If only I'd seen something that was more radical, or maybe this is too far out for me, maybe I should find something safer."

Those are all valid approaches, and I feel very proud of the conservative labels that I've done. I did a label for Creighton Hall Winery, and the idea was to make it look like a book binding. I was thinking of Masterpeiece Theater. The owner is a British gentleman, very refined and cultured, expensive wine and everything. So, I really wanted something that if you lined the walls of the library with bottles of wine instead of books it would have the initial appearance of being a library of bound volumes. That was a very conservative approach. We designed a crest for him that was based on the lion and the unicorn of the British emblem, yet it worked *real* successfully. That was what he wanted. It was the perfect solution for that project.

The idea in that initial design presentation is to present a range of options, so there will be this feeling of a wealth of riches. There are so many great options that I don't know what to pick. That's what really motivates me, knowing that I'm going to have to sit down with someone whose opinion I respect, and sell him on the idea that we have these great labels and they're exciting and they're just going to take the world of wine marketing by storm.

I illustrate these ideas as best I can with what I call comps or comprehensives. I try to make these little representations look pretty close to the finished product. That's one thing I've always really liked, the craftsman-like job of creating these little beautiful one-of-a-kind artisan-like representations of what the printed work will be. That's where I am the most present, in making those one-of-a-kind pieces that capture the imagination, and to get people excited about the job. Once it's on the bottle, it's almost not my work any more.

It's the little presentation labels that are really the heart of where I am in the whole process that's exciting to me, knowing that I have to present these to people, and that they have to be good, and eventually stand up in the market place. It's that inter personal relationship of having to prove yourself to another person directly, one-on-one, and all you have are these little representations of your skill and your taste and style to convince them. So, it must have something to do with the way that I relate to people in general, because it's like I don't have enough confidence to present an idea just on the strength of my word. But if I can create some little thing to show them, they'll think that I have the ability or expertise or what-ever. It's like I can really prove to people that I can do something, and these little label reproductions are the proof of my own expertise in some way. So that's the crux of my personal involvement with it.

So that's the way I'd make a presentation to somebody. I find out what they want, to my own perception, and usually I can hit it pretty well. If I make eight to ten reproductions, there are usually three or four that end up being real promising. I encourage people to make a selection of no more than two or, if absolutely necessary, three primary directions that they want to develop.

I stress that we only need to come up with one perfect label, and if they like the typography from one label, and the illustration from another, and texture or color from another, then we can blend them. What we're looking for in this label presentation is a variety of ideas that are all expressed and all available, and may or may not be adaptable in combination.

Then, taking that group of ideas that I've generated in discussion, I'll go back, come up with some more ideas of my own, and graft the two together. In a way, I'm trying to find out what works best as well, and I don't know until I see it either. Nobody knows what's going to work until it's on paper. Some of the things that sound the best come out the worst, and some things that don't really sound like they would be that productive turn out to be great. So when people say, "How would it look if we put this here?" I have to say I have no idea how it would look. Everything's different. Everything's unique, and part of creating a wine package is that in a sense, you will be seeing things that haven't been seen before.

The tricky part of the process is getting the ideas translated into print. You never really know how it's going to work in the final printed process, because everything does change when it's actually being mass produced. Producing one single finely-honed piece for a presentation is a lot different than creating something that can be mass produced in thousands and thousands of images and still be equally successful.

Sometimes, it turns out to look better in that way. Sometimes it doesn't. So, that's tricky. Making sure that it can be accomplished, and that it will make the transition is the biggest challenge at this stage... to make sure that you understand the printing process, and the foiling and embossing process and everything, so that whatever magic you hopefully have captured doesn't evaporate once it's been reduced to its finished form. You don't want there to be a sense of disappointment there. It should always look better in its finished form.

Getting a label produced is fairly straightforward, actually. It's a matter of producing a mechanical piece of art, and double checking to make sure the size is okay. They're sort of technical details, but it's always a rush at the end. The main thing is to be sure that you have the time to put it together solidly and explain it.

If you have a great idea at the core of a project, then the technical aspects can shift and change, but the essential idea will come through and may be better than you planned. Accidents can be fortuitous as well as detrimental. I never feel like my master plan is the one and only perfect way to achieve success. There are a lot of things that can happen.

On one project, for example, we were looking at the way I had shot this picture, and the separator said, "What happens if we flip this over, and just use the angle coming in from the other side?" And I think it really looks better. But that wasn't in my plan, it was something completely unpredictable, just an accident, and it worked better.

Printing is an art, in and of itself. I try to be involved all the way through the final printing process. I'm always there when it's printed, when it's foiled, and there to oversee the color separating. I do all this myself, because each possible area for foul-ups is also a possible area for improvement.

If you're there looking at it and keeping an open mind, and you realize that it's never too late to make a change for the better, then you can use that to your advantage. I try to use those technical areas and other people's expertise for the betterment of the project, rather than letting it just disintegrate on you. I've found that people can be real helpful giving you their own unique perspective. In fact, you have to have the strength to reject advice if you don't feel it's appropriate, but being open to advice is a big part of what I do well.

Q: What do you do when the client picks what you're convinced is the wrong choice?

Well, that has happened. I try not to present anything that I would not feel comfortable with. I may feel that it's a lost opportunity, but usually there's a certain safety factor in going with something that someone really likes, even if it's not adventurous.

At its worst, designing a wine label is a very good way to earn a living in an interesting fashion working with interesting people. Some labels just turn out to be that kind of a label. They aren't a personal break through. They're not anything that's going to shape the future of graphic design, but they may work very successfully within a given context.

Even if a label is really good, if people aren't comfortable with it, then it's going to be hard for them to sell it. I can't promise that they will receive accolades on the strength of my design that will eventually make them comfortable with the label. If I've given them a recommendation against their wishes, and it turns out well, then that's fine. But I don't really feel comfortable doing that, because it's something that they have to ultimately be responsible for in the decision making process, 'cause it's their wine.

At its best, you should be looking into the wine through the label. You should get some key to what it is about the wine that's unique, not in a literal sense, but in the sense that it has a personality. You can also see a label in the context of being a covering, where it seems to conceal a lot. I try, even in a conservative label, to have that quality that you're looking within the product, that it's a window on the wine as opposed to a covering. In other words I want my labels to reveal, not conceal.

Sometimes ideas that are rejected by one client may resurface in some later context. I've never really just turned a good idea around and showed it to somebody else. It always evolves, but the core of the idea can remain. It it's something that stays with me, and it's something I will show to somebody else perhaps in a different form.

Years later it may surface and then find its real home. So, I don't ever consider these opportunities to be lost forever. I just think of it as not quite the right time or place for it. I always have hope that my good ideas will eventually find a way to see the light of day.

Q: What is it about your job that just pisses you off?

I'm frustrated with my own inability to do everything perfectly. It's so easy to screw up in some little area. It seems like all the great work you've done is at the mercy of petty details. I wish there was some way I could rise above that, or to become so skillful that I didn't have to worry about it, or have time to double and triple check everything. It really bothers me when things go wrong. I feel personally responsible for that.

There's nothing about having people come to you and outline interesting projects and ask you to use your imagination that I find frustrating. That's an unending source of joy to me. Sometimes, I feel like I'm not up to the challenge, and that's a little frightening, to feel you don't really have what it takes to do the best job. No one really understands the complexities of anybody else's job. So, I can't complain that people don't give me enough time, or enough input, or understand the kind of difficulties that my job entails. That's something that is not unique in any sense to my job.

Q: Do you ever get to the point where you say, "I don't want to do this anymore?"
Yes, definitely. Trying to do too much, just being pressured from the outside. Too many projects, too many deadlines. Too many things that have to be done without the time to do them, but that doesn't happen often.

Every now and then, the flow of my work gets to be such that there are a bunch of things that are all due at the same time, and that can be very difficult to handle, because everything is predicated on the whole process going smoothly. When everything goes wrong at the same time, there's just not enough time, and not enough of me to go around. But the frustrations lie mostly with my own inability to schedule properly and to leave enough time for everything.

The creative process is something that you can't rush, and I don't pretend that this is much of a creative inspiration type thing. I'm never just sitting, staring into space waiting for inspiration. My job is such that I can look through reference books, go to the library and follow little trails of information. Those are the things I love about what I do. I love searching for clues. It's detective work, and I really get a kick out of that. Once it leaves my office, that's the source of my greatest frustration, when

232

it's in somebody else's hands and things start to go wrong.

Q: Do you think your clients have any real understanding of art and design or the technical process of printing?

In a sense, I don't consider anybody to really have to know anything about art and design or the technical process. I don't consider them to be responsible for that. In terms of marketability, wine people have a wide variety of experience with other people's products, and the kind of products that get noticed and that have shelf appeal.

A good package sort of speaks for itself. They're little personalities, and in fact, the personality of the wine package extends to the sculptural form, the fact that it's got a cap and shoulders and a neck, and it's this little anthropomorphic figurine, in a sense. The sculpture is a little personality, and it expresses itself.

In the label, it's like meeting somebody when you see a wine for the first time. You don't have to know this person to know that they're interesting. It's like you want to know the wine. For people to understand art and design, or the technical aspects of production, is not as important as to see something that uses the technical and artistic spheres to create something of interest. The interest has to be there, regardless of their level of expertise.

Q: In terms of the whole job, what gives you the biggest charge, the most satisfaction?

There are two things. First of all in the personal context, having people just absolutely delighted with what I've done, feeling that it's better than they dreamed. That's my goal in every project, and I always feel a real sense of disappointment if people say, "Well, this is good stuff. We'll find something good here."

I'm not going for "good." I'm going for a real big pat on the back, and I want people to tell me that this is great, and that their lives will never be the same because of what I've done for them.

I also really like to see my work reproduced in print, and to see it in magazines, and to have people all over the world looking at what I do. In a sense, I feel it's getting out into the flow of commercial graphic art. Other graphic artists see it, and the world is never the same. That's real exciting to me too, seeing my work out there in the world and influencing the course of events.

Q: How much of this philosophical approach that you have to design is tied to your studying anthropology?

I don't think very much of it, actually. It gives me hope that you can define the world on your own terms, and it it's successful, then it becomes its own reality. I don't think that's anthropological, except in the sense that anthropology makes you realize that civilization is a very thin veneer over an extended history of mankind, and that our impulse toward beauty and touching and appreciation and warmth and sharing are all very deeply rooted. In the same sense that a wine label is a very thin layer around a wine bottle, our civilization is a very thin veneer around what really makes human beings human, and that wine somehow has the ability to penetrate to the depths of human beings and make them aware of things that go beyond the superficial aspects of life as we tend to construct it around ourselves. I think anthropology does that.

I've always thought that you learn more about an era from the ticket stubs and receipts and the paper wrappers than you do from the works that were officially recognized as being works of art. I think that's the key to past cultures, and I like to think that I'm providing keys to future historians concerning our contemporary culture.

It's very much tied into that. It goes back in an archaeological sense to the early surviving wine vessels as well, which provide a real continuity in history, starting in Mesopotamia and Greece and Rome and everything has always been very closely related to Egypt. Wine and vineyards and wine bottles are all surviving relics from past civilizations. I think that the continuity of the past is one of the things that gives depth and a meaning to what I do. In a sense, it's very superficial, but anything that has that type of lineage has to have some validity. Again, it's just a means of explaining something and rationalizing it, and telling us that what we're doing is significant. But in a world where all things are relative, who's to say that it's not?

Actually, when you asked the question, I said that anthropology didn't have much to do with it, but as I'm thinking and as I'm talking, I may not be making a lot of sense, but I am sort of getting an awareness that it may have more to do with it than I had thought.

Q: Do you ever drink a wine, then look at the package and say, "This package is wrong for this wine."

That's interesting. I tend to take the package pretty much as something that will outlive the wine, in the sense that the bottle will be there after the wine is consumed. I tend to think of the package as being more important than the wine, to tell you the truth, because it's going to be there from vintage to vintage. If my theory of immortality is correct, this is the artifact that the future archaeologists will unearth, and the quality of the wine itself is almost secondary to the importance of the packaging.

I hate to say that to a winemaker, but in order to really do my best job, I have to feel that what I do is the most important aspect of the whole process. So, in a way, it's disappointing when a wine isn't as good as my packaging, but in that case, I've certainly done my best to upgrade the quality of the product.

Q: Why do you think people associate wine with romance?

Romance is a self-perpetuating myth. If you believe that romance exists, it can be created. I think that the sense of wine as a mystery to be unlocked, something that you open and sample, is inherently theatrical in that the appreciation of wine exists as a process through time. It has an introductory phase. It has a phase where you become mutually acquainted. If it's really good, it has a phase where you are extremely relaxed, similar to meeting a person.

The romance parallels with getting to know a wine, unlocking its mysteries, appreciating it at its best, and then eventually relaxing and becoming comfortable with it.

From a consumption aspect, you incorporate it into your own personality. It's almost a religious significance that involves a symbolism with the sun and the earth, masculine and feminine strength.

The process of creating wine evolves from this dual nature of the sun and the earth, creating and growing something that resonates on a mystical level. I've noticed that feeling, in an era where people don't go to church a lot, the feeling of people going into a winery, and it opens up above you, almost cathedral-like, and you stand and you consume the wine, and you almost see these fabled wine makers as saints in a secular religion or something. The depth of wine itself is very conducive to the kind of mystery and symbolism that's conducive to romance.

I'm real interested in this idea of history and immortality, the symbolism of wine packaging, and the sculptural form of it. The fact that in wine packaging you have the cork and the paper, which are wood. You have the foil, which is metal. You have the glass bottle. Then the wine is a combination of the earth and the sun and the rain. You have a focus for a microcosm of the world, and the fact that those all come together in the wine package can make it a very magical sort of thing.

It's a whole that's definitely greater than the sum of its parts. I think the opportunity to blend those elements is a unique opportunity. I don't feel I've really done it right, yet. There are many times when I feel the best wine package has no label on it at all, just the pure sculpture, the pure sculptural form, but when you see the empty bottle you feel like there's a little something missing, and I have an opportunity to add color.

I guess one of the main reasons I do this is that I just like doing things once, as opposed to doing the same thing over and over again. I never really thought about it, but that must be why I keep getting excited about these new projects. Every time a new one comes along, there's that chance to do something new.

Order Form

Postal Orders: Send your check or money order to:
Wine Patrol Press
P.O. Box 228
Vineburg, CA 95487

Or fax (707) 938-9460

Please send _____ copies of **Cold Surveillance** to:

Name: _____

Address:_____

City:_____ State:_____Zip:_____

Price: The price of the book is $9.95 for the first copy, but only $8.95 for each additional copy. Buy several, and give them to others you think would like to meet Jake Lorenzo.

Sales Tax: Please add 7.75% for books shipped to a California address.

Shipping: Book rate: $2.00 for the first book, and $0.75 for each additional book in the same package.

Amount enclosed_____